THE

Vow

THE VOW

How a Forgotten
Ancient Practice
Can Transform
Your Life

ED GUNGOR

THOMAS NELSON
Since 1798

NASHVILLE DALLAS MEXICO CITY RIO DE JANEIRO BEIJING

Published in Nashville, Tennessee, by Thomas Nelson. Thomas Nelson is a trademark of Thomas Nelson, Inc.

Thomas Nelson, Inc. titles may be purchased in bulk for educational, business, fund-raising, or sales promotional use. For information, please e-mail SpecialMarkets@thomasnelson.com.

Unless otherwise indicated all Scriptures are taken from the HOLY BIBLE, NEW INTERNATIONAL VERSION (NIV) © 1973, 1978, 1984 by International Bible Society. Used by permission of Zondervan Bible Publishers.

Other versions used:

The New King James Version (NKJV), © 1979, 1980, 1982 by Thomas Nelson, Inc., Publishers. Used by permission. All rights reserved.

The King James Version of the Bible (KJV).

The Living Bible (TLB), © 1971 by Tyndale House Publishers, Wheaton, IL. Used by permission.

The Message (MSG), copyright © 1993. Used by permission of NavPress Publishing Group.

New American Standard Bible (NASB), © 1960, 1962, 1963, 1968, 1971, 1972, 1973, 1975, 1977, 1995 by The Lockman Foundation. Used by permission.

The Contemporary English Version (CEV) © 1991 by the American Bible Society. Used by permission.

The Amplified Bible (AMP), Old Testament. Copyright © 1965, 1987 by Zondervan Bible Publishers. Used by permission. And The Amplified Bible (AMP), New Testament. Copyright © 1958, 1987 by The Lockman Foundation. Used by permission.

The *Holy Bible*, New Living Translation (NLT), copyright © 1996. Used by permission of Tyndale House Publishers, Inc. Wheaton, Illinois 60189. All rights reserved.

New Life Version (NLV) Copyright © Christian Literature International.

Library of Congress Cataloging-in-Publication Data

Gungor, Ed.
  The vow / by Ed Gungor.
    p. cm.
  Includes bibliographical references and index.
  ISBN 978-0-8499-1911-4 (trade paper : alk. paper)
    1. Commitment (Psychology)--Religious aspects--Christianity. 2. Vows. 3. Promises--Religious aspects--Christianity. 4. Christian life. I. Title.
BV4597.53.C56G86 2007
248.2'5--dc22
                                                    2007033069

Printed in the United States of America

08 09 10 11 12 RRD 6 5 4 3 2

to

Michael, Robert, David, and Elisabeth

"Behold, children are a gift of the LORD."
Psalm 127:3 (NASB)

CONTENTS

I'm taking a risk in this writing. I'm letting you in on a journey that is probably more theoretical than practical at this point in my life. I've been on this trajectory for only a few years, but it has proven to be so provocative and engaging, I had to write about it. The bottom line is I want a deeper relationship with God, and I want to be more radical in my participation in the kingdom of God—not because I have to in order to be "saved," but because we all get one shot at this gift called "life," and I want to live it as large as I can for God. That's how I stumbled onto the path of vow-making. My journey began with a boat-load of questions, and I still have a bunch—they are different ones, maybe better ones, but still questions. But I think that's OK, and I think there is fodder here for some great, worthwhile conversation.

Have you ever been hiking on a trail and noticed an old, faint footpath wandering off the main trail deeper into the woods? I love those. I can hardly resist the temptation to explore. Sometimes those tracks yield adventure, and sometimes they simply wind right back to where you started (which makes them more a waste of time than anything else).

Making vows has been one of those less-traveled trails for me. I came to Christ when I was a teenager, and I've been on the God-trail for almost forty years (I'm officially an old guy). About six years ago I noticed this little pathway of vowing as I was casually reading the book of Acts. Though vow-making is virtually an unknown practice to us moderns, it was a very familiar practice to the ancients who have gone before us. Vows are simply promises we make to consistently practice actions that communicate grace and strength to our souls. Consequently vow-making helps foster a robust spiritual life—a kind of "steroid," if you will, for spiritual formation and discipleship. As I have wandered this direction, it has been both intriguing and empowering, and, yet, on another level, just plain dangerous (legalism always broods in the shadows of *any* intentional faith practice). But I really think it's leading somewhere. That's the *why* of this writing.

In my book *Religiously Transmitted Diseases: Finding a Cure When Faith Doesn't Feel Right,* I addressed the issue of how legalistic religion is *bad* religion and the kind that sullies the innocence of faith. But not all religion is bad. Religion born from God's initiative (versus the human-centered kind) is pure, undefiled, innocent, and powerful. Man-made religion looks a bit like the God-initiated kind (closely enough to fool many), but it is a *diseased* faith. And, sad to say, it is a disease that is easily transmitted to others. To be sure, vow-making *is* about religion, but it's about the "pure and faultless" kind described in Scripture.[1]

INTRODUCTION

The word "religion" comes from the Latin *religare*, which means "to tie fast" or "to bind to." Good religion is doing the things that tie you to God's graceful, unconditional love—it is choosing to respond to that love with a resounding *yes* in your soul.

A Misplaced Gem

In May 2005, to the delight of Bach lovers everywhere, an unknown composition by Johann Sebastian Bach was discovered by a classical music scholar in Germany. There was no evidence that anyone had ever heard this composition, which was a two-page handwritten aria dated October 1713, when Bach was twenty-eight years old. The piece had been tucked away in a box of birthday cards given to Duke Wilhelm Ernst, whom Bach served as court organist. Bach enthusiasts did not *need* this piece of music to enjoy and love Bach, but from their perspective they had discovered a misplaced gem.

I feel like "vow-making" is a misplaced gem. Except in the lives of a relative few, it has been hidden—"tucked away" for many years. Christ-lovers do not need this gem in order to enjoy and love Jesus, but I believe its discovery will delight the heart of all of us. Before I discovered it, I was not lost, but I am richer for the find. I think you will be too.

—Ed Gungor

1. What Is A Vow?

Praise awaits you, O God, in Zion;
to you our vows will be fulfilled.
−Ps. 65:1

I was breezing through my devotion time one morning and hit a verse that got me rubbernecking. (Ever rubberneck while reading the Bible?) I was reading the book of Acts when this verse snagged me: "He had his hair cut off at Cenchrea *because of a vow he had taken*."[1] It was my morning rush hour (I needed to get to an appointment), so I couldn't stop to investigate, but I knew I was going to have to return to the scene later to figure out why the great apostle Paul—the New Testament grace man—participated in a vow in the first place. Other than getting married or becoming a priest or a nun, I thought vowing was some kind of antiquated, Old Testament *thingee* that I was sure Jesus had abolished.

When I came back to the text later, I discovered another verse in Acts that had never caught my attention in regards to the "vowing" practice. Paul was asked to accompany to the temple four other believers who had "made a vow."[2] I had never noticed it before, but these New Testament Christ-followers were making vows!

As I dug deeper I discovered that the practice of vow-making was actually commonplace in the early church. Making vows, it turns out, was about as popular as prayer and worship gatherings. Scholars claim the making of vows was practiced by ordinary people all through Israel's history, as well as by adherents to most religions in the societies surrounding Israel.[3] The popularity of making vows is peppered all through the Bible. For example, King Joash refers to "personal vows" in 2 Kings,[4] and the Lord instructs Moses about a "special vow" people could choose to make as a part of their worship.[5]

This vowing practice continued in the early church and was not at all considered unusual, as is evidenced by the passages that did not include further explanation, including the reference to Paul and the other disciples cited above, and from records from the first century. Tony Cartledge claims this "shows that vow-making was an important element of popular or 'folk' religion throughout the ancient Near Eastern world of the first millennium."[6]

What Is a Vow?

Vows are love-promises we make to God. They are "descriptive of the thanks of the pious"[7] and have been called "acts of generosity toward God"[8] throughout church history. Vows are simply our own unrequired, promised love-acts directed toward God and the cause of his kingdom. They are not unlike the simple, unexpected gestures of love and kindness couples show each other in order to make their relationship special (we'll come back to this later).

Vow-making was popular through all Jewish history. So much so that the Jews were guilty of being overly zealous about them—they made too many and did not take them as seriously as they should have. Though vow-making has always been seen as something voluntary (vows are never mandated in Scripture), once a vow is made, it is sacred; it must be kept. The Hebrew word for a vow is *nadar*, which is connected with the word *nazar*, meaning "to dedicate." Solomon warns, "When you make a vow to God, do not delay in fulfilling it. He has no pleasure in fools; fulfill your vow. It is better not to vow than to make a vow and not fulfill it."[9]

Because the Jews tended to make vows rashly and then forget them after the emotion of piety wore off, there was actually a special evening service dedicated for people to back out of the vows they had made during the previous year! It was a kind of "reset button" for Jewish vow-makers, and it took place in the synagogue the night before the Day of Atonement. It was called *Kol nidre*. The service opened with the words, "All vows, renunciations, bans . . . which we vow and swear and ban and bind upon our souls, from this day of atonement until the [next] day of atonement which shall come for our welfare—we repent them all; they shall be solved, remitted, abolished, be void and null, without power and without validity. May our vows be no vows."[10] The fact that a service like this even existed shows us the historical popularity of vow-making.

While the Old Testament assumes vows are a natural part of religious life, the New Testament is basically silent about them. That doesn't mean they are invalid, and may actually imply that the discussion of them in the Old Testament is enough to make a case for participating in them. Vows were so commonplace that the New Testament writers saw no need to justify their presence in worship practice.

Jesus and Vow-making

The one time Jesus addressed vow-making was when he needed to correct those who had vowed resources to the temple that they should have used to support their elderly parents (a biblically commanded responsibility). Jesus was not opposed to vowing here, but he clearly points out that a voluntary vow cannot nullify or obviate a biblical rule, which in this case was honoring one's father and mother. Precisely because vows are voluntary, they can never usurp a biblical command.

Though Jesus does not side against vowing in general, he did speak against "swearing" or making "oaths" in Scripture. Jesus said, "Again, you have heard that it was said to the people long ago, 'Do not break your oath, but keep the oaths you have made to the Lord.' But I tell you, do not swear at all."[11] But there is a difference between making a vow and swearing an oath. Webster's defines a vow as "a solemn promise," and defines swearing as "an act to invoke the name of [God] in an oath." Jesus was against folks' invoking the name of God in an oath. Let me give you an example.

When I was a boy, we kids would sometimes use the phrase "I swear to God!" when we were trying to convince each other we were telling the truth. Most young boys have integrity issues as well as a penchant for deception, so we would occasionally need to bring up God's name as a backup to our word. In essence we were saying, "You may not believe me on my own merit, but I'm bringing in God to back me up on this!"

Adults are far less likely to openly swear by heaven, but I can't help but wonder if we aren't just more sophisticated at it. Ever see a businessperson with the Christian fish symbol prominently displayed on his or her business card? I've seen it on the cards of plumbers, carpenters, car salespeople, and so on. I've even seen lawyers and doctors use it. (I live *smack* in the buckle of the Bible belt.) I know some are trying to honor God by doing so, but I have often gotten the impression that many of these individuals are trying to use God to give them more credibility than they have earned on their own. When I see business cards or Yellow Page ads like this, I can't help but feel it's just a little *fishy* and I think, *I appreciate that you are a Christian, but are you qualified to do the work you do? Do you have a good reputation? Is your customer service satisfactory? Or does your fish imply God is siding with you and so should I? Are you trying to make me feel (consciously or not) that if I don't use you I am resisting God in some way?*

This is the kind of thing I think Jesus was addressing when he forbade swearing. He said, "Simply let your 'Yes' be 'Yes,' and your 'No,' 'No'; anything beyond this comes from the evil one."[12] He was telling folks not to bring God into the equation to prove they are telling the truth or to prove they should be trusted. Instead, they just need to have a reputation that speaks for itself that they are good at what they do. People will see a difference in the way you do things, and they will ask you about it. Peter writes, "Always be prepared to give an answer to everyone who asks you to give the reason for the hope that you have."[13] If you live a God-honoring life, people will notice and ask you about it. *Then* give glory to God, which means you should probably redo your business cards.

Vows and the Church

Actually, vows were commonly practiced throughout church history. It wasn't until the Reformation in the 1500s that leaders like Martin Luther began to speak of vows in a derogatory way.[14] However, it is important to note that this attitude was probably jacked-up a notch or two by the fact that the Reformers wanted to push off from the authority of the vow-friendly church at Rome.

Luther took the stand that the only important vow made by believers is the one made at water baptism. The "baptismal vow" is a promise to believe in Christ, to hope for eternal life in him; it is a promise to live one's life in accord with the ordinary norms of good conduct. He argued that this was an "all-embracing" vow. He saw all other vows as secondary at best.

Though Luther was willing to tolerate vow-making, which, again, evidences their popularity, he thought little of them. John Calvin, however, insisted that vows had merit and could be engaged in to reinforce the weakness of the human will or to express one's gratitude toward God.[15]

The Greatest Vow

I agree with Luther that the granddaddy of all vows is our baptismal vow. Scripture says when a person comes to Christ, "we were all baptized by one Spirit into one body."[16] The church has historically demonstrated this "spiritual baptism" through water baptism. When we begin to declare Jesus Christ as Lord of our lives, our baptism into Christ becomes an all-embracing vow that our whole life belongs to God. And this vow is life changing. Paul writes, "If anyone is in Christ, he is a new creation; the old has gone, the new has come!"[17]

On a purely theological and philosophical level, Luther's position seems to be the best: being baptized into the body of Christ means Christians are pledged completely to Jesus Christ—lock, stock, and barrel. Declaring Jesus as Lord means we belong to him, period. And since the baptismal vow commits us to a total conversion of our will to God's, it seems obvious that any secondary or lesser vows would be pointless. However, on a practical level, our baptismal pledge to Christ's lordship seems to get lost in the shuffle. Think of it this way. When two people marry they go to an altar and commit before God to have and to hold each other in love and respect till death parts them. But no couple expects to accomplish this task just because of the words they promised at the altar alone. Unity—two becoming one flesh—is no small task. Most couples recognize they will have to work in special ways toward understanding and loving each other before they will experience the promise they committed in their vows. They know it will take time and a great deal of effort to mirror what was promised at the altar. And as they wrestle through various issues, they will need to make smaller commitments—secondary promises or lesser vows, if you will—in an effort to "work out" the unity they committed to achieve.

This is the same role "lesser vows" have in our Christian experience. They do not replace the commitment we made to the lordship of Christ in the moment we were baptized, but they help us work out that baptismal vow in our daily experience. Remember Paul's words, "Continue to work out your salvation with fear and trembling."[18] *The Message* translates this verse: "Redouble your efforts. Be energetic in your life of salvation, reverent and sensitive before God." I'm suggesting that vow-making helps us to do this in specific, concrete ways. I think this is what Calvin meant when he took the position that vows had merit and could be used to reinforce the weakness of the human will or to express one's gratitude toward God.

Lesser Vows

I think it is obvious that we need more than the one-time baptismal vow for discipleship and a robust Christian faith. Scripture calls us to "Devote yourselves to prayer, being watchful and thankful."[19] In another place Paul urges that saints should "Be careful to devote themselves to doing what is good."[20] The word "devote" is actually derived from the word "vow." Its etymology is the Latin word *devotus*, which is the past participle of *devovEre*, from *de-+vovEre*, which means "to vow."

A "devotion" to prayer or good works would be an example of believers participating in a secondary kind of vow—a lesser vow than the baptismal vow but still one that is encouraged in the Scripture. I think lesser vows help us to fulfill the call to pursue the holy—to do more than just sit on our "blessed assurance."

And there are oodles of texts that call us to consider deeper commitments in our faith. We are called to be "zealous for good deeds,"[21] to "walk in a manner worthy of the Lord," to "please him in all respects," as well as "bearing fruit in every good work and increasing in the knowledge of God."[22]

Then there's this challenge from Paul for believers to train like Olympic athletes:

> You've all been to the stadium and seen the athletes race. Everyone runs; one wins. Run to win. All good athletes train hard. They do it for a gold medal that tarnishes and fades. You're after one that's gold eternally.
>
> I don't know about you, but I'm running hard for the finish line. I'm giving it everything I've got. No sloppy living for me! I'm staying alert and in top condition. I'm not going to get caught napping, telling everyone else all about it and then missing out myself.[23]

This is *not* casual Christianity. This is bore-on commitment; this is deep consecration. And though there is no suggestion that one must be this passionate or consecrated to be saved (salvation is the work of God, not the result of human perseverance or diligence[24]), I do think feeling a deep, compelling need to consecrate oneself back to God—to give God more than he demands, which is the point of vow-making—is a natural reaction for those who have been deeply touched by God. There is something in us that echoes the psalmist's cry, "The LORD be magnified."[25] When God is magnified, it means he gets bigger in our lives!

The Why of Vow-Making

Truth be told, I love God less than I want to. Jesus talked about loving God "*with all your heart and with all your soul and with all your mind and with all your strength.*"[26] I'm not sure I love him with *all* that. Oh, I have my moments when my faith is white hot—an occasion of worship at church or at the apex of a morning devotional—but those moments don't seem to last.

I want to love God more than I do. I want to love God enough to be willing to do what saints who have gone before me have done: to be willing to give all my possessions to the poor and follow Jesus;[27] to be stoned or sawn in two or slain with the sword;[28] to be willing to wander about in sheepskins and goatskins; to be destitute, afflicted, or tormented;[29] to be willing to go to a foreign country and live among the poorest of the poor like Mother Teresa; and so on. God hasn't asked me to do such things, but I want to be at a place in my soul where he knows (and I know) that if he should, there would be a resounding *yes* in me.

I'm not talking about ordinary faith here. Nor am I talking about something that is required. I'm talking about loving God in unnecessary, unrequired ways. There is a required love: we're supposed to love God enough to receive what he has freely given us in Christ. We're supposed to love God enough to face the cross so we don't ignore what Jesus did for us. Salvation is found there. And that is where our journey of faith begins. This is really all that is necessary or required by God as far as loving him is concerned. But that doesn't mean there isn't more.

There is plenty of room for believers to love God extra—room for us to be caught up in an infatuation with the holy. I'm not saying we should try to love him extra in order to make him love us more—he loves us period, not in response to what we do or don't do. I'm not nervous about how God feels about me. I constantly focus on the fact that he loves me incautiously and recklessly. In fact, I find great comfort knowing that he knows every stupid, silly, mean, ill-motived, and outright sinful thing about me and, yet, he still pursues and loves me. But I don't want to just think about that; I want to respond to that. I want to love God more than I do—to be eager, even passionate, to go the extra mile.[30]

I am also aware that I cannot love God more on my own. Loving him is a reflex to my discovering his love for me, as John expressed when he wrote, "First we were loved, now we love. He loved us first."[31] When you visit the doctor and he hits that spot just below your knee (or on your elbow), there is a "reflex"—an autonomic muscle response. Unless you're diseased or disabled, you can't help kicking your leg. The same is true here. Unless you're deeply diseased with sin and deception, the more you hear about and catch a glimpse of God's love with the eyes of your soul, you can only respond with love back toward God. It's a reflex.

I think the secret of loving God more is to order our lives in such a way that we intentionally and consistently experience the presence of God. The more we see him, the more he hits that spot in our souls that causes the reflex of love back toward him. Loving God more is possible only if we intentionally face

God more. I think this is why the psalmist prayed again and again, "Restore us, O God; make your face shine upon us, that we may be saved."[32] I want more face time with God. I want to forget him less. This journey of faith is all about gazing at the one who is invisible, and I want to journey well. David prayed, "One thing I ask of the LORD, this is what I seek: that I may dwell in the house of the LORD all the days of my life, to gaze upon the beauty of the LORD and to seek him in his temple."[33]

So how does one order his or her life to intentionally and consistently experience the face of God? There are many ways, but I have come to believe one way is by participating in the ancient art of vow-making. Pete Greig writes, "For those of us wishing to go deeper in our commitment to Christ, an exciting discovery is awaiting us in the grace of vows. . . . These are treasures with which the Patriarchs, the Apostle Paul, and Christ himself were clearly familiar, and yet have been all but lost by contemporary culture."[34]

By participating in vow-making, our lives become a channel of love back to God. Vows are born from an intentional desire within believers to allow God's Spirit to penetrate the various facets of our lives in real time and space. They are promises that hope to shape our futures for the glory of God. The vow serves as a commitment on our part to *respond* to God's love—never to *earn* it. Vows position our souls to love God in a tangible way—transporting our faith out of nebulous piety into actual practice.

The vowed or dedicated life is not an end in itself; it is a spiraling process of ever-expanding openness and movement toward God. Vowing helps us let go of anger and the negative aspects of our human nature and to hold on to the grace of

God—this transforms all that we are and do. In vowing we say no to the world as it is, but our no isn't where we stop. Our no implies a yes to something more. We say yes to creating love in the world where it is not and to sharing in the *missio Dei*, the mission of God. We end up no longer using the world for our own self-interests; we purpose to seek God's will and goodness for a hurting world. We seek mercy instead of retribution, reconciliation instead of rejection and alienation.

Vows give us conviction about the kind of life we are to live, clarity about our role in the world, and a sense of corporate mission and ministry. There is a critical and prophetic power about them. We are not just believing differently; vows cause us to do and live differently. And a life dependent on grace is a prophetic life.

I think the Holy Spirit is constantly calling the church to be prophetic; that is, he calls the people of God beyond their basic understanding of Scripture into deeper insights and newer ways of expressing that Word in their lives. The church finds herself constantly surprised by the Spirit. Jesus claimed, "The wind blows wherever it pleases. You hear its sound, but you cannot tell where it comes from or where it is going. So it is with everyone born of the Spirit."[35]

Of course, this comes with some anxiety. Every time any new "way" is discussed in the church, we have to examine if it is from God, from man, or from the devil. Saints all through history have had to wrestle through doubts and fears as new movements or emphases emerged. In fact, this is one of the signs that something really is of God—it disturbs. God often likes to shake things up. The writer of Hebrews declared, "See to it that you do not refuse him who speaks."[36] He goes on to say, "[God] has promised, 'Once more I will shake not only the earth but also the heavens.'" The words "once more" indicate the removing of what can be shaken—that is, created things—so that what cannot be shaken may remain.[37] Remember the prophets? John the Baptist? Jesus himself? The Reformation? The Great Awakening? Every time God does something new, it shakes things up.

I'm not suggesting vow-making is going to become a "movement" of any great significance in the church. In fact, I'm suggesting nothing of the sort. However, I *am* saying that if you are on a quest to love God more, it is worth taking a stab at things that may be unfamiliar to you. As a committed "vower" personally, I can tell you vowing has added a whole new dimension of joy and freedom to my journey of faith.

But beware. Vows have nothing to do with earning favor or love from God. If you never make a vow to God, he will love you no less. Nor do vows make you a better Christian—vowing is more than a pathway to a "good Christian life" or personal perfection. Vows are simple; they are the unnecessary ways we love God *back*—ways that make us a people "after [God's] own heart."[38] It is precisely the voluntary and non-essential nature of vowing that gives it its power. This kind of living is about focus, which is the essence of purity. This kind of living causes us to be saltier and brighter in the world, attracting both converts and persecutors. It makes us different, even subversive to the status quo—aliens, if you will.[39]

Richard Foster writes, "In our day heaven and earth are on tiptoe waiting for the emerging of a Spirit-led, Spirit-empowered people. All of creation watches expectantly for the springing up of a disciplined, freely gathered, martyr people who know in this life the life and power of the kingdom of God. It has happened before. It can happen again."[40] My prayer is that vowing will help to that end. I am not trying to establish some kind of elitist group of vow-makers; my intention is to share a lost art that can help us moderns pledge ourselves to God in a fresh new way.

Vows are evidence of a desire to follow Jesus without reservation. They are choices that eliminate others—pre-decisions that symbolize the direction that will ground one's entire life. And they open the door to divine adventure.

Let's see how, next.

2. There's Got to Be More

"Somehow we all know that to play it safe
is to lose the game."
—Erwin Raphael McManus[1]

When most think about God they think of rules, commands, judgments, and wrath—with the cherished counterbalance of grace and forgiveness sprinkled in. In American evangelicalism the goal of faith appears to center on believing the right thing—the gospel. But if belief is the *only* goal of the gospel, then once a person believes, life is *futureless*. We've finished the race when we cross the finish line of "spiritual enlightenment." I'm not suggesting that belief isn't critical or the place we must start—it is—but isn't there *more*? Is it possible that God's dream for human destiny is more than just believing a message?

It seems to me that Jesus and the early church were less focused on believing in something to "get ready for eternity" than they were driven to create a community of people who lived differently, precisely because they believed something unique. Their belief was an alternative vision of reality that demanded a nonconformist value system different from the one being heralded by the religious and political contexts they found themselves in. These were a people who testified to the life, death, resurrection, and ascension of Jesus Christ by embracing a new dimension of living—one committed to death, if need be, in order to fulfill the *missio Dei*—the mission of God—in the world.

This bunch believed that the events of Jesus's life, death, and resurrection—and the story that those events carry forward into the present—really do make sense of life. These were men and women who aligned themselves with that story, which made them different. They belonged to Jesus Christ, who was present to live in and through them.

But relatively few think of Christianity as a call to enter a new kind of living—a life jacked up with adventure, mission, and divine destiny. Faith, for many, is nothing more than fire insurance from hell, some acquiescence to rule-keeping (it's the least we can do), and a safety net of forgiveness when we break the rules. On this view the human experience of faith isn't much more than a life of stumbling and bumbling around, "holding on" to faith the best we can till Christ sees fit to bring us home.

But what if the Christian life is supposed to be more than that? What if it is a calling for us to step into something larger than ourselves? What if God is inviting us into something more than legalism and rules? What if he is inviting us to participate in some kind of *divine quest*?

Something "Tookish"

In J. R. R. Tolkien's classic book *The Hobbit*, Bilbo Baggins lives contentedly in his home at Bag End, Hobbiton Hill, until one spring morning the wizard Gandalf visits him. Gandalf, sensing that there was a hunger for adventure beating secretly in Bilbo's heart, said to him, "There is more to you than you know."

Bilbo, it turns out, was part of the Took clan, on his mother's side. They were the ancient defenders of the Shrine. Gandalf knew that though Bilbo may have inherited the easygoing nature of the Hobbits from his father's side, his Tookish thirst for adventure would eventually lead him to go beyond the safety of the Shrine into the adventure that would save the world.

I think God put something "Tookish" in all of us. Erwin McManus writes, "There was a voice screaming inside my head, *Don't sleep through your dreams!* Ever heard that voice? It calls you like a temptress to abandon the monotony of life and to begin an adventure. It threatens to leave you in the mundane if you refuse to risk all that you have for all that could be."[2]

I think there is something in us that wants to be part of saving the world. *True*, we have those things we inherited from Adam that make us cower and lunge into survival-and-protection mode, but we also have a drive in us that wants to make a difference, that wants to glorify God. We don't have to settle for being bean-counting legalists who only color between the lines; we can be spiritual pioneers, adventurers who dare to explore what a life fully committed to God can really look like.

A Time–Critical World

God has invited us to be participants in establishing his kingdom in the world. God does not force that participation on us;

we must choose it through our obedience. Truth is we don't have all that much time—one life, one shot. This ought to freak us out a little. We ought to be a little crazy about seizing each day, trying to jam them full of as many right choices and as much Holy Spirit activity as we can possibly say yes to. Jesus said with a palpable sense of urgency, "As long as it is day, we must do the work of him who sent me. Night is coming, when no one can work."[3] We need to keep that sense of urgency alive in us. The psalmist said, "Teach us to number our days."[4] In other words, it's good for us to think about the fact that we are going to die. Get that; it helps! *You are going to die.* So am I. We are going to expire, croak, become dust-lickers. Living life with this awareness isn't being morbid; it makes us live better.

For me, this is one of the main motivations for vow-making. Vows are ways we come to God to commit to something that is uncommanded, but for which we feel an impulse of duty because of the suspicion of divine destiny. We vow because we want to love God diligently—in ways that exceed his commands. And because vows are directed to God himself (and not just resolutions within one's self), they are commitments with a shot of Tabasco in them. They are not to be entered into lightly.

As we will see, vows can be attached to *anything* one wishes to commit to—from developing a more consistent prayer life to becoming a better spouse; from desiring to become more biblically literate to being a better manager of one's sexuality; from focusing on making life more sacramental to allocating specific time and resources to social justice issues; and so on. Vows can vary in duration from a single afternoon to a particular season to one's entire lifetime. All in all, vows help us to intentionally embrace anything we feel the Holy Spirit may be nudging us toward in view of bringing God's kingdom to bear in our world.

I want my days to matter. I don't want to be guilty of living in the sin of *sloth*. "Sloth" is defined as the lack of desire to perform work or expend effort. It is one of the historical seven deadly sins. Sloth, in the context of spiritual life, means we don't make it a priority to do what we should or to seek for the grace to change what we should in ourselves. We become apathetic, which means we have no *feeling* or motivation to act. We see this sin present in Israel as Jesus calls out: "O Jerusalem, Jerusalem, you who kill the prophets and stone those sent to you, how often I have longed to gather your children together, as a hen gathers her chicks under her wings, but you were not willing! Look, your house is left to you desolate."[5]

For Christians, spiritual sloth sometimes means we really don't care what the Bible teaches about something, so we put off reading or asking about it. Sloth keeps people from participating in challenging spiritual experiences or events. It's easier to spend our time glutting our souls with TV than working to engage with people or ideas that call us to action, such as loving our neighbor, helping the poor, or telling the truth.

Having faith and experiencing salvation does not mean you are participating in the *missio Dei*. I think receiving Jesus is different from being an apprentice of Jesus, his mission, and his ways. Being Christ's apprentice suggests you are not just believing in the message of redemption and experiencing personal forgiveness—that is certainly where it begins, but that is not where it ends. Following Jesus is an adventure in being countercultural. It is being on a mission to change the world. This is beyond simply dedicating one's life to faithful service in order to build up a local church congregation, its programs, numbers, and facilities. This is about a change of heart, about us putting our skin in the game of bringing God's justice into an unjust world. Vows help us stay "in the zone" of fervent obedience.

But obedience is not the fruit of simple human effort; it is the fruit of *grace*. This is why all vows are really vows into *grace*.

3. VOWING TO GRACE

*I pray the Lord grant that you observe all these things
as lovers of spiritual beauty, giving forth
the spirit of Christ in the holiness of your conduct,
not as slaves under the law but as free people
firmly established in grace.*

—Augustine

I'm a lousy legalist. Usually when I hear others talk about serious discipleship—things like making a deeper commitment to Christ—I feel like someone has just thrown a heavy, leaded X-ray apron on my soul. Commitment is a scary enterprise for me (and "vows" are commitments on steroids!). I was never a Watchman Nee fan.

The problem is I'm not very good at committing to things. My capacity for commitment has always been tragically flawed. For example, I can make a resolution to lose a few pounds, deciding I'm not going to eat any more pie. But I like pie. So, in spite of my anti-pie commitment, if I am offered pie after deciding to live pie-free, my no-pie resolution usually dissolves into an only-*one*-piece-of-pie resolution. This leads to the only-one-*more*-piece-of-pie resolution, which then carries me until no more pie exists.

The Vow

Because of my lackluster history with commitment, even my commitment to loving God has yielded spotty results. I can't tell you how many times I have made a no-holds-barred, no-nonsense commitment to Jesus Christ. I've herded forward hundreds of times in altar calls to do business with God. I think I felt a lot like a professional wrestler in the WWF, preparing for a match—huffing and puffing, slinging spit, waving my arms, and trying to convince myself that I was going to leave that altar with a bigger and stronger love for God—one that would help me "whoop" whatever came into the "ring" of my life.

But those hyped-up promises to God never lasted. Sure, they started out hopeful, but my commitments were like the squint you have when you walk out of a movie matinee on a sunny afternoon. You experience a pretty good glare at first, but it quickly wears off. I would come away from those altars squinting like a pro. But after a few hours, or by the next morning, it wore off and I was back to my old patterns of living.

But in the church circles I grew up in, there was constant chatter about "commitment." In fact, most of the preaching I heard was about commitment. "If Jesus died for us, we must decide to live for him" was the touted credo. Every serious believer I knew talked only about committing to surrender and sacrifice—the deeper life. "Hard" became the badge of spirituality. Being a mature Christian meant being big on commitment, but I just couldn't get it. Things were so deep for me that I found it too hard to breathe.

Trust me. My journey into a lifestyle that includes vow-making has nothing whatsoever to do with a heavy, deeper-life faith suited for the few, the proud, the "Marine" Christians. I could never make the cut. I am not good enough. Certainly not consistent enough. I don't have enough willpower. I'm a vower because I've discovered vowing is perfectly suited for the average Joe and Jane, the frequently inconsistent, the weak, often foolish, and sometimes loser. My kind of crowd.

So, how does a flawed committer like me ever succeed at vow-making? What I have discovered about vowing is that, if done accurately, it keeps me trusting God in a way that causes *good works* to emerge in me—as sure as apples emerge from an apple tree. The secret to successful vowing is realizing vows are commitments to faith in God and his work in the human heart, not to human performance. Vows are not human-centered commitments, they are "God-centered" ones—ones founded on grace.

Discovering Grace

Grace is an amazing thing. There is no way it makes sense. It is God lovingly chasing us when there is no reason for it. When the psalmist caught a glimpse of it, he cried, "This is too much, too wonderful—I can't take it all in!"[1] Neither can we. It may resemble the natural kindness and love that families and married couples share, but it plunges far deeper, and it is way more unconditional and deathless.

Paul prayed that his friends would have the "power to understand, as all God's people should, how wide, how long, how high, and how deep his love is."[2] It takes power to understand God's love and grace toward us—God has to help us see it.

I totally get how some think all this is too good to be true.

How can it be? How can God be so reckless about giving to us when we are so good at being so bad? But that is exactly what he is like. We matter to him, and there is nothing we can do to alter that. Understanding this is the foundation for Christian vow-making. We vow into grace, not human perfection.

It was Jesus who said, "If a man remains in me and I in him, he will bear much fruit; apart from me you can do nothing."[3] This verse is saying that being fruitless, doing "nothing," is par for a human experience apart from a vital connection with Jesus Christ. In other words, "nothing" is what God expects from fallen people who haven't yet learned how to rely on the grace of God.

Think about this: God never expects you to perform for him in your own strength. Your responsibility as a believer is simply to come to him, to remain in him, to find ways to connect with him, and he said that approach would naturally cause you to bear "much fruit." He does not expect you to bear fruit on your own.

Understanding this verse was a watershed moment in my thinking about faith. I began to realize that the whole "commitment" thing that I had been trying to perfect for years was misdirected. It was a hoax. God was never after my *performance;* he was always after my commitment to *trust* him. In the end he still expects me to live righteously—all of us are called to live holy lives—but trying to do this through human energy alone ends up producing a "right" that is dead wrong. Paul claims this is how the Jews missed the power of the gospel as a nation when it was first proclaimed. "Since they did not know the righteousness that comes from God and sought to establish their own, they did not submit to God's righteousness."[4] An attempt to establish a self-righteousness out of trumped up human piety never ends up being *right*, and it produces little more than a soul-perverting pride.

Christian righteousness is only secured by faith.[5] But having faith, which is placing trust in another, feels a little like suicide to fallen human beings—it's scary. It's so much easier to shift the footing of our faith from God and his working in our lives to our own performance. But acting for God was never part of the program; we are to act with God. He never intended for people to be solo performers, acting independently of a direct connection with him, any more than manufacturers create appliances to work independently of a power source. But he did create us to work *with* him. Paul writes, "So here's what I want you to do, God helping you: Take your everyday, ordinary life—your sleeping, eating, going-to-work, and walking-around life—and place it before God as an offering. Embracing what God does for you is the best thing you can do for him."[6]

Holy Living

Does God expect us to live holy lives? Absolutely! But there is a caveat. It is *how* we live a holy life that is the million-dollar question. Do we attain holiness by what we do or by what is done to us?

This has everything to do with *origins*—where does holiness come from? The Old Testament Law called for goodness to come into our lives through Olympian human effort. But there is a problem with human effort: it is infected with sin! Paul wrote, "The law always ended up being used as a Band-Aid on sin instead of a deep healing of it. And now what the law code asked for but we couldn't deliver is accomplished as we, instead of redoubling our own efforts, simply embrace what the Spirit is doing in us."[7] New Testament grace says "goodness" is a fruit of the Holy Spirit that comes to us through simple faith.[8] On some metaphysical level, we participate in God's goodness (the divine nature[9]), and there is transformation. Paul describes the effect of the commingling of the divine with the human heart: "He brings gifts into our lives, much the same way that fruit appears in an orchard—things like affection for others, exuberance about life, serenity. We develop a willingness to stick with things, a sense of compassion in the heart, and a conviction that a basic holiness permeates things and people. We find ourselves involved in loyal commitments, not needing to force our way in life, able to marshal and direct our energies wisely."[10]

According to St. Augustine humans can "will away" all we want, but it will not produce consistent right-living because sin has broken the effectiveness of the human will. This is the worm that has curled its way into the apple of the human condition. For Augustine, human freedom cannibalized itself when humans chose to sin. This means our ability to commit is too damaged to be fruitful in any spiritual sense. It's as if the will has a kind of built-in vicious cycle for self-love, which is too strong to push past self-interest—at least not without help. And the will cannot unscramble itself from this condition. Augustine says, "Who can disentangle this most twisted and most inextricable knottiness? It is revolting; I hate to think of it; I hate to look at it."[11]

Human effort alone is inefficacious. This is why Paul cries, "What a wretched man I am! Who will rescue me from this body of death?"[12] He was talking about the whole dilemma of wanting to do right but always ending up doing wrong, a concept most of us understand all too well. Amazingly, Paul was comfortable with the revelation that he was a "wretch" and that there was nothing he could do about it on his own. He seems to be comfortable with the notion that we humans cannot fix ourselves. He answers his question concerning where rescue comes from by crying out, "Thanks be to God—through Jesus Christ our Lord!"[13] We need something other than our nature to will rightly, and the only successful therapy is divine grace administered to us by the Savior Jesus Christ.

But this grace needs to be pursued on our part. Divine grace will not strangle human will. This is where vowing into grace aids us. Grace is only experienced in the course of an intentional movement toward God, though the Christian considers even this movement a result of grace. Augustine says we must run to God, but that God will "set our feet" in the right way so we can run to him.[14]

There is complexity here. And the apostle Paul states that complexity well, "But by the grace of God I am what I am, and his grace to me was not without effect. No, I worked harder than all of them—yet not I, but the grace of God that was with me."[15] He's claiming that grace is not experienced in the absence of free choice, but he's also stating that it is not obtained by free choice either. This means that every human being has freedom of choice, but not everyone has the inner ability to use that choice wisely—to choose rightly. Choosing rightly is an "inner liberty" that requires a peppering of grace (or the direct action of God). But once this grace is experienced it enables a person to enjoy choosing and doing the right thing, which is giving one's self to the love of God.

An analogy may help here. If the will were an eye, sin has blinded it. Grace gives the eye the ability to see. It illuminates and reveals. It gives the non-functioning eye—blinded by sin—the ability to see and thereby to function rightly. Through grace, the will's blindness is healed. We no longer have to stumble in the dark.

If we are having trouble making right choices, we must push harder into grace. Grace is what transforms us—it is where we are given sight. Once we see, choosing rightly and living holy is within our grasp. Vow-making can help us more consistently pursue and participate in the grace of God.

But how does one "vow" into grace?

4. How We Vow into Grace

You will pray to him, and he will hear you,
and you will fulfill your vows.
—Job 22:27

Grace brings hope to humanity. Grace is the idea that God gets in the mix of the average person's world. It means things can be different, our lives can be transformed. The word "grace" comes from the Greek *charis*, a word ancient Greeks would have used when raising a glass in the bars of their day to say, "The gods be with you." It was a casual greeting with a modern equivalent being "Have a good day." But the phrase was powerless because there are no *gods*. The Christian writers commandeered the word to refer to God's unmerited favor, implying that "if God is with you, you really will have a good day!" Faith in God would actually bring change.

And that is exactly what grace does. It changes things. It changes people. The task at hand is to figure out how a person with *your* unique personality and mind-set can best tap into grace. For me grace is most easily accessed as I ponder Scripture. As I wrestle with texts, grace dawns inside me. My wife, Gail, taps into grace as she sings and worships. Others touch God's grace most by getting together with other believers, by retreating into times of solitude, or by one of the other many spiritual practices modeled in Scripture and church history. And there are a bunch of them: study, worship, celebration, service, prayer, fellowship, confession, submission, solitude, silence, fasting, sacrifice, and so on. (For more, see Appendix B). Once you find the pathways that help you experience grace, you can vow to consistently practice those pathways in order to stay under the influence of grace. This is what I mean when I say that New Testament vowing is really vowing into grace.

When Paul wrote about grace, he warned that it could be "in vain" as far as our lives are concerned—that means grace can be present but have no influence over us.[1] *Yikes.* Again, grace demands participation. We need to work grace into our lives, which means we must tangle and wrestle with the spiritual discipline of seeking God. I'm convinced that the free, available, abundant grace of God is only secured as we *weary* ourselves in pursuit of it. God says, "You have not called upon me . . . you have not wearied yourselves for me."[2] This is at the heart of vowing to grace. Grace is free, but it is not secured without personal cost. Paul said grace was huge in his life because he "worked harder" with it than most had.[3]

Are you working to ensure grace is not "in vain" in your life? Vow-making is about promising to move into the ways that make you aware of God's mysterious presence, while asking him to invade your thinking, your reasoning, and your will with his grace.

Over the years I have discovered that certain things communicate grace to my soul more powerfully than others. For me grace is most easily accessed as I do contemplative things (such as prayer, meditation, solitude), so I'm now participating in a vow to do what is referred to as the Daily Office (see Chapter 12 for more detail). The Daily Office is an ancient way to pray and meditate on Scripture several times throughout the day. The Scripture says that Daniel intentionally practiced withdrawing from activity to observe a time of prayer and adoration three times a day.[4] The psalmist David did it seven times a day.[5]

I refer to them as "God Breaks" and I generally do them four times a day. (I started with seven but have found four to be just about right!). My goal with these "God Breaks" is to balance the responsibilities of my life with prayer and meditation in such a way that there is a continuous awareness of God in the back of my mind as I work through the day.

Here is a sampler from Psalms that captures the kind of spiritual attitude I try to emulate during my breaks throughout the day:

> *Thank you! Everything in me says, "Thank you!"*
> *Angels listen as I sing my thanks.*
> *I kneel in worship facing your holy temple*
> *and say it again: "Thank you!"*
> *Thank you for your love,*
> *thank you for your faithfulness;*
> *Most holy is your name,*
> *most holy is your Word.*
> *The moment I called out, you stepped in;*
> *you made my life large with strength.*[6]

There are a number of other vows I am currently committed to, but the point is, they are not vows to human performance but vows to encounter grace. We vow to stand under the spout where the grace pours out for us. Vowing is for those who have discovered the impulse of grace that causes us to say yes to the right things and no to the wrong ones. Some of us weaker, less-than-best saints have unearthed the joy in grace making weak people strong. We've found that the power of God dawns in the human soul at the point of grace. So we are running after it.

Lesser Heroes

The 1999 movie *Mystery Men* was the story of a trio of super-heroes with fairly unimpressive superpowers. The opening scene is in Champion City, a metropolis in a slightly altered, comic book-style reality, where costumed crime-fighters (many with mediocre powers) are in oversupply, to the point that many of them are out looking for work.

Three such individuals are The Shoveler (played by William H. Macy), who can wield a shovel pretty well; Mr. Furious (Ben Stiller), who has the "ability" to get very, very angry; and The Blue Raja (Hank Azaria), a self-described "effete British superhero" who throws forks and spoons but refuses to use knives and wears a green turban (the running joke being that, despite his name, his costume has no blue in it whatsoever).

This motley crew arrives to foil a robbery in an old-folks home by a similarly inept band of villains. They are largely incompetent at what they do and are quickly upstaged by Captain Amazing (played by Greg Kinnear). This guy is a gen-uine superhero, arriving just in time to save the day and completely upstage the wanna-be heroes, who are treated as a joke by the police officers, villains, civilians on the scene, and Captain Amazing himself.

There are a lot of Captain Amazings in the evangelical church. I am not one of them. If you are, you are going to be disappointed with how I approach vow-making. I am not remotely interested in helping you look or become more amazing than you already are. This whole writing is for those of us who do less well, who have unimpressive powers—hardly super—yet still want to change the world. I want to give us permission to stop with the gaudy costumes and fake accents and to start living authentic lives.

So . . .

Vowing into grace takes the horror out of the "shoulds" and "coulds" of the Christian faith and aborts the quest for perfectionism. When you taste grace, you begin to freely and joyfully engage in good works. Paul says, "The grace of God teaches us to say 'No' to ungodliness and worldly passions, and to live self-controlled, upright and godly lives in this present age."[7] Then, he claims, we become "a people that are his very own, eager to do what is good."[8]

Scripture asserts, "God does not respond to what we do; we respond to what *God* does. Our lives get in step with God and all others by letting him set the pace, not by proudly or anxiously trying to run the parade."[9]

We vow as a promise to trust God's grace to work in us and to work out the struggles and opportunities of the future. By participating in a graced vow, we are testifying to the idea that we believe God really does want to engage in the human experience and to establish his rule through us—we invite God's action into our history. And this is the activity that results in fruitfulness.

True and False Vow-Making

In one of the churches I pastored, there was a single guy who lived rather promiscuously but wanted to honor God with a holy life. As I urged him to pray about the things that triggered his inappropriate behavior and how to begin to trust God's grace to break that up, he told me he thought the real solution was to quickly find a girl to marry. He thought entering a marital vow would be what he needed to stop his promiscuous behavior. I told him that was the wrong reason to marry. Vows are not intended to be promises of what we hope to be, but promises of who and what we are to one another. He needed to get control of his life *before* he was ready to enter a marriage vow.

The same is true in our vow-making to the Lord. Vows are only valid in areas you have *already* learned how to live by the power of grace. They are promises to remain consistent; they are not to be used to scare ourselves into being something we are not. If you try to use vows or promises to God to make yourself a "better" Christian—because you are having a hard time being consistent with your prayer life or Bible study, or you feel guilty because you miss church because of laziness, or you are having a hard time saying "no" to sin, and so on—you are setting yourself up for failure.

Don't think to yourself, *Maybe if I make a vow before God it will give me the extra "oomph" I need to get my life in order. Maybe if I make a vow to God it might scare me into doing what's right.* It is wrong to vow to do things you know you have not been able to do before. Vows are not to emerge out of a "cross-fingered" hope that you can promise your way into becoming more consistent. Remember: we are not to "swear by heaven" when our yes is not strong enough to stay a yes and our no is not strong enough to remain a no.

This is what I think James was getting at when he wrote, "Above all, my brothers, do not swear—not by heaven or by earth or by anything else. Let your 'Yes' be yes, and your 'No,' no, or you will be condemned."[10] If you can't sustain a yes or a no via the combination of effort and grace, you are not ready to vow. We vow, not to try to get to the place where we can keep our word, but because we have had enough experience with grace to understand how it works. We vow to stay in the place where grace is efficacious on our behalf—where it is not in vain.

Personal Victory

Before we talk more about vowing into grace, let's sidebar on the issue of personal holiness for a bit. Paul urges believers to live transformed lives in which we no longer conform to the pattern of this world.[11] Moral development is necessary. It is part of being an adult, and in the beginning of our spiritual lives our emphasis needs to be here. Young Christians, like natural children, are given more to emotions and impulses than to reason and wisdom. So the first step in truly becoming a mature spiritual person is to learn how to live morally astute lives by surrendering to the inspirations of the Holy Spirit and to the Word of God.

Either the Bible is true or we are being lied to. It says you and I are free from the dominion of sin. Paul writes, "Could it be any clearer? Our old way of life was nailed to the cross with Christ, a decisive end to that sin-miserable life—no longer at sin's every beck and call!"[12] Then he said, "Sin is no longer your master. . . . Instead, you live under the freedom of God's grace."[13] I think the only reason the redeemed of God (that's us—Jesus's apprentices) get slammed and controlled by sin is because we have not yet discovered the rhythm of grace that will suspend sin's pervasive influence over us. But even when it looks like we are losing the sin battle, the fact remains that we are free and sin has no right to control us! Sin's power is broken as we pursue the grace that lifts and frees us.

Paul declared that God is committed to our victory over sin. He said, "You have never been tempted to sin in any different way than other people. God is faithful. He will not allow you to be tempted more than you can take. But when you are tempted, He will make a way for you to keep from falling into sin."[14] Jude wrote, "There is One who can keep you from falling and can bring you before Himself free from all sin."[15]

There is a way for you to live free from the tyranny of sin—God has a 911 escape plan for you. You do not have to be bound. Sin no longer has the right to dominate you. If you are bound, don't justify it or learn to live with it—that will only destroy your capacity to participate in the life God affords. Most likely you haven't found the right blend of classic disciplines—worship, giving, prayer or examen, small group interaction, meditation, silence, service, fellowship, Bible study, devotional reading, centering prayer, Scripture memorization, *lectio divina* (Google this, it's cool!), confession, journaling, and so on—that will impart sufficient grace to you. You don't have to live so that your past failures predict your future. You don't have to live under controlled destructive behavior.

Path to Moral Freedom

In the first stages of our spiritual growth, the emphasis is on what the person can do—his efforts with help from God—in order to establish the proper chain of command within him or herself. This is a place of deep wrestling and usually takes years. If one focuses too much on the human element, she will not reach the bar of holiness. If she thinks it is purely the work of God, she will also fail. Holiness, it turns out, is not the work of God or humans alone; it is the result of a coworking between the divine and the human. And it takes lots of time, effort, patience and persistence to learn how that works. (Plus, it needs to be worked out within the context of community—more than just you!)

Here is where Scripture plays such a critical role. John pens, "I write to you, young men, because you are strong, and the word of God lives in you, and you have overcome the evil one."[16] Jesus used Scripture to help him fight his battle over the "senses" as he was tempted in the wilderness. He claimed, "Man does not live on bread alone, but on every word that comes from the mouth of God."[17] Scripture not only communicates God's standard, it comes packed with life. As you meditate on it you are infused with life—the very breath of God.[18]

At this stage, human effort is learning to work with grace

and grace is working according to human effort. And some confusion is inevitable. During this phase of gaining mastery over one's self (even with the aid of grace), our efforts will appear very much the same as that of the pagan stoics—their literature actually proves helpful at this point in a person's spiritual formation. The stoics held that each person needs to be deeply committed to their respective "duty" no matter the circumstance, no matter how one feels about it—you just do what you are supposed to do, period. That is why so many of the early Christian spiritual masters drew on the writings of the stoics to instruct and inspire their own disciples.

It is OK to discover the limits of your human effort as you work hard to establish a consistent walk of holiness. This is not bad unless we get deceived into thinking that we can grow in grace by this effort—we cannot. Though it is not bad to try hard, we must recognize human effort is not a cure-all. We must discover its limits, use what we can from it, but then push past it into the grace of God.

You need to discover and successfully practice the right blend of work and grace. And you need to be content with experiencing failure in the process. Failure is not the end of the world for believers. We have great promises like that in 1 John 1:9: "If we confess our sins, he is faithful and just and will forgive us our sins and purify us from all unrighteousness." The text says God "is faithful" to forgive us—that means he is more faithful to forgive us than we are "faithful" to sin—you can't beat God at this.

Why does God make forgiveness this easy? Because he doesn't want us focused on failure as we are trying to figure out how to live well. He knows it takes time to develop moral excellence. It takes time to learn how to dominate and conquer the things that challenge our freedom in Christ, whether it be the inside world of our instincts, passions, and drives, or the outside world of the things that threaten or entice us. But we must learn. We have to be in possession of our "land" before we can surrender it. And so the first war you must wage is the war on *self*, and then you can surrender that "self" to God.

That's why the spiritual journey begins with us, as it were, on top looking down on our motivations and actions. Later, as we experience more freedom and consistency, the direction of our faith gaze will change. We will be less conscious of controlling ourselves—our emotions, motivations, passions, and actions—and more conscious of being surrendered. We begin to find ourselves at the bottom, looking up to God, whose inspirations have become our law for living, whose love has become our motivating force. Hence, though John writes that the young men need to be strong and need to wrestle with the evil one using the word of God, he says that the older believer has settled into knowing him who is from the beginning. One looks down doing battle with grace until grace produces sufficient victory to look up. (On paper these two stages of development look like they happen sequentially, but in reality they both happen in tandem in the believer's life, with a complexity that is beyond the scope of this writing.)

The point here is that vow-making is not applicable at the early stages of Christian development—effort and grace discovery are. And it is only after you have learned to find the balance between human effort and divine grace to master your lower nature that you can think rationally and be prepared for making vows (except, perhaps, you could vow to "find the balance").

The Vow

Vows are *not* designed to help you become more consistent in your faith. Vows are not a "hothouse" for spiritual development. However, once you learn how to walk with mastery, you can enter vows freely and effectively.

Vow Dates

When you find an area you experience grace in and want to vow into, you should spend sufficient time testing how the vow will really impact your life—to make sure it consistently communicates grace to your soul and does not become a soul-crushing legalism. I experimented with the Daily Office for several months before vowing to participate in it. I discovered it consistently poured grace and strength into my soul—so I vowed to practice it. It's currently a one-year vow for me. I'm suspicious that it may turn into a lifelong vow, but I think you need to experiment with a vow temporarily before you make it permanent—you need to "date" it first.

I'm considering making some dietary vows for my health to honor God with my physical body,[19] but I'm still working on adjusting my diet with simple grace and accountability before I ever start vowing in that department. Vowing should never be used to help us successfully do what we believe we should be doing—obedience and surrender to grace are what should accomplish that. We can only vow to grace—we can only vow to do what we have learned to successfully do by his grace without a vow!

That's why we do not participate in vowing before God in an attempt to prop up our own inconsistencies. We cannot make vows to get ourselves to do what we have not been able to do by God's grace heretofore. (That would be another version of "swearing by heaven" and is a kind of false-vowing.)

When you vow into grace, you are "committing" to live in the experience and fruit of God's favor and blessing. This kind of vowing is about you saying yes to what it cost Jesus his life to make available to you. Paul says it best, "Now God has us where he wants us, with all the time in this world and the next to shower grace and kindness upon us in Christ Jesus. Saving is all his idea, and all his work. All we do is trust him enough to let him do it. It's God's gift from start to finish!"[20] You may have experienced grace and seen its fruit in your life in the past, but that doesn't mean you are living under grace *now*. Paul said that grace is a daily, now thing. Grace isn't a yesterday, or last-week, or a when-I-first-came-to-Jesus experience. It is like the manna God provided the Israelites in the wilderness—it had to be fresh to be edible. You need fresh, just-from-the-oven "grace bread" to experience the transformation it gives, which is the point of vowing into grace.

However, vowing is not about solo human effort and legalism, and immature or struggling believers who do not yet understand being controlled by the rhythms of grace should not try to participate in them. If you are new to "grace" thinking, stay away from vowing for a season; it will only hurt you. Vowing is for the believer who, though not perfect, understands the impulse of grace and how to cooperate with that impulse, and has experienced the grace that transforms.

5. Vowing into Personhood

As for any other vows, let each of us make any we wish.
—Augustine

When we were little and being assertive about what we wanted, my mom used to tell us, "You kids think you're people." Most of us agree that when we become aware of ourselves and our freedom, we become "people." It is in the *exercise* of freedom that we become unique persons. This suggests that we develop our personhood in degrees—one can "become" more of a person than one was previously. How? Personhood emerges as we recognize our freedom and take responsibility to make good use of it.

When you were little, you oriented yourself to what was going on in your culture and environment—you longed to "fit in." You were hardly a person yet—you were not even aware of what it meant to really choose because all your choices were being made for you. You simply accepted everything you were told by your parents, teachers, or trusted adults, and were not really conscious that you had any say in the matter. You were unaware of "options." At that time in your life, there was only one real way to live—only one way to eat or dress, only one place to live, one school or church to attend. You had no knowledge of being able to choose the kind of life you wished to lead. You simply accepted what you were told and adjusted to what you experienced. It was only when you became aware of yourself (which occurs in the period we refer to as adolescence) that you realized you had options and choices. This is when it dawned on you that you could personally adopt whatever attitudes and values you wanted to, versus only embracing those mandated to you, and you discovered what it means to be "free." This is when you began to become fully a *person*.

Gail and I have been married for over thirty years and we've raised four great kids: Michael, Robert, David, and Elisabeth. Though it took lots of time and effort—and was jammed with wagonloads of challenges—we loved raising kids. We loved teaching them general stuff like how to play fair, how not to take things that weren't theirs and to put things back where they found them, how to say "I'm sorry" when they hurt someone, how to not hit each other, how to love others enough to share, how to wash their hands and flush the toilet, and how to love and trust in God. We raised our kids to be responsible, contributing God-lovers who cared for more than themselves.

As important as it was to us for our kids to embrace the general responsibilities of life, that was not what delighted us most as parents. The real parenting fun was in seeing their individual personalities emerge—when their uniqueness started to stick out. We wanted them to fit in, but we also wanted them to stick out in ways that were unique to them. We wanted them to share similar values as ours—get them committed to the Golden Rule, basic sanitation, devotion to God, and so on—

but we wanted them to live beyond our rules and expectations—we wanted them to soar into being their own persons.

Our oldest boy, Michael, grew up to be a contemplative, accomplished musician and songwriter, who has a delightful lightness in his soul, rock-solid integrity, and a contagious laugh. Our second, Robert, is the life of the party. He's our "envelope pusher"—he is always just a tad south of completely inappropriate but delightfully and hilariously so. He is also an amazing musician and brilliant web designer who actually gets paid an insane amount of money for his talent—a comfort to his aging parents. David is our ambassador—he makes us look like better parents than we actually are. He is a great communicator, also a musician (my wife claims all the musical talent came from her side of the family, but you and I know she's just making that up), and serves in pastoral ministry. Elisabeth, our baby, is a sheer delight. She is beautiful, shockingly witty, a dancer, and has a heart for others that is selfless and sacrificial. Our kids are all so different, and they are so not by our parental design but by God's design and their own free will—by the choices they have made.

What makes us fully "persons" in our own right is to realize that we can create ourselves by the choices we make. God created us as human beings and chocked us full of potential, but we create ourselves (in full cooperation with God) as individual persons. Who we are as persons is the cumulative effect of all the free responses we have given to life—to circumstances, to those around us, and to God. In a sense, when we make our choices, we are making a name for ourselves.

Ever notice how hard it is to remember someone's name until you get to know him or her? Personhood is determined by the content of how one lives. We create the kind of persons we are by the free choices we make—what we choose to do and not to do. If you fail to realize this, you fail to enter into full possession of who you really are. You fail to understand the potential and power of your freedom. You are not yet a person.

Our Personhood in Christ

There is a season in our spiritual development where we must orient ourselves to the Christian faith, where we need to find out where we fit in. In this stage of faith we don't need to try to wrestle with what it means to have choices, because we need to learn what is universal for all of us. When we first come to Christ we need to learn how to dialogue with God; it's called prayer. Then there's the Bible. It is a mystical book that fills the believing heart with life, wonder, grace, power, and comfort. All Christ-followers treasure the Bible.

Then there is learning to fit into God's family. When you decide to become a follower of Jesus you become a member of the whole family of seekers on earth—God calls it the "church." It's very important for all believers to learn how to find their place in our spiritual family, which Paul calls the body of Christ. He contends it must, like any body, function as one. Paul wrote, "The way God designed our bodies is a model for understanding our lives together a church: every part dependent on every other part. . . . You are Christ's body— that's who you are! You must never forget this. Only as you accept your part of that body does your 'part' mean anything."[1]

In addition to these basic Christian principles there is the important aspect of *discipleship*. We must all learn how to grow in grace, to say no to sin, to walk in love, to live grateful lives, to adopt a Christian work ethic, to practice hospitality, to live by faith, to overcome evil with good, and so on. These are the things all of us need to learn and practice as fully devoted followers of Jesus Christ. But mastering these practices doesn't mean we have learned to express our individual personhood in Christ. In fact, I'm not sure there are all that many people who understand that Christianity is more than just universalized activity—there's room for individual graced expression.

Maturity in Christ is not realized by embracing the general responsibilities of the Christian life. It is realized when you start choosing things that *you* enjoy or feel passionate about and your individual "spiritual" personality (influenced by your connection with Christ) emerges. Maturity is realized when, of free will, you begin to move toward your unique passions, gifts, interests, and callings.

We need to fit in, but we also need to stick out in ways that are unique to us as individuals. We all share similar values, but if we want to experience the graced self-expression of being full persons in Christ, we need to live beyond rules and expectations. Vows serve to facilitate this!

You can certainly enter into spiritual "personhood" without ever making a vow, but vowing gets you specific about participating in the things we believe are valuable—they help make your faith expression concrete. In vowing, faith becomes more than a vague feeling of loving God and desiring to help people. Though we still participate in the general responsibilities of the Christian faith common to all believers, vowing helps us to intentionally love God the way *we* want to love him.

The Power of Unnecessary

There are some things that are necessary to the survival of any friendship or loving relationship. It is important to be honest, to respect the other person, to manage your differences, to communicate and listen (never assume), to solve problems, to apologize, to cooperate, to commit to meeting each other's needs, and so on. These are the necessary things for all healthy, growing relationships. But it is the *unnecessary* things that turn a mediocre friendship into a great one or an ordinary marriage into an amazing love affair. And it's the unnecessary things that give a relationship its own unique structure, style, and culture—its own DNA.

When I first met my gorgeous, to-die-for wife, Gail, I did all the necessary things to win her over: I was courteous; I smiled; I treated her with respect; we conversed, and so on. But the more interested I became, the more I started doing "extra" stuff that got her to notice I existed. Instead of a friendly glance, I gave her lingering looks. (FYI: a "lingering look" is more subtle than the awkward, ogling, stalker-stare that scares women away.) I found the things that made her giggle and worked *extra* hard to keep her giggling as much as possible. As the relationship deepened, I found *extra*-cute nicknames for her, spoke to her in an *extra*-special, sweet tone of voice—in fact, the whole relationship took on a particular pattern of *extra* looks, gestures, and codified words that made our relationship special. The necessary relational obligations mentioned above continued; they were *necessary*. We needed them (as all relationships do). But it was the unnecessary things that made Gail's and my relationship unique. They enabled us to find a specific rhythm that made our relationship ours—that evidenced we were, in fact, falling in love.

The necessary relational actions are foundational because they give every relationship structure. But it is the unnecessary gestures that give relationships that special *something:* it's the extra dab of mustard in our family's baked bean recipe or the splash of white vinegar in our navy bean soup that make it uniquely ours. And it's the "secret ingredients" we bring when we are cooking up love that cause us to believe, "My recipe is best!"

After thirty-plus years, Gail and I are still committed to the extra stuff: calls during the day, flowers and kind words, help around the house, listening ears and open communication, bringing each other coffee in the morning, her playing with my hair (what's left of it) or my massaging her feet while we watch TV (she has nice feet), playful talk and loving glances, "drive-by" love-touches as we pass each other throughout the day, the occasional snuggle to each other's faces. Though these things are technically noncompulsory, they add something wonderful to our relationship. I think a love without the "special" is boring . . . maybe even dead. A relationship that only follows the rules may appear neat, organized, and predictable, but don't kid yourself—order and predictability are the principle characteristics of rigor mortis.

Vows, God, and DNA

As I stated earlier, our relationship with God carries some "necessary" things with it. But our relationship with God can be defined by more than these "necessary" efforts—we can love God in unique ways, in ways we want to love him. Just as every couple and every friendship is different with its own peculiar relational DNA, we can have the same experiences with God. How you love him can be different from the ways others love him. This is what vowing affords us.

Vows help us make our relationship with God unique, private, and personal. Individuals initiate vows, and they do so without the oversight of religious leaders or the regulation of biblical mandate. Vows belong to the impenetrable personal religious space of the believer. Here we have the opportunity to speak and commit ourselves directly to God without mediation or regulation by any religious authority or biblical command.

Vows are not regulated in Scripture because they are not required. Hence, they serve as a kind of love language between just God and us—a language that is framed out of our longing to express love to God. In his book *The Five Love Languages*, Dr. Gary Chapman claims every person has a primary emotional love language based on their unique psychological makeup. He suggests that there are five basic love languages by which people feel and express love. They are: words of affirmation, quality time, receiving gifts, acts of service, and physical touch.[2]

This means every couple in love has a unique mode of communication—a way they love to love. Vows bring this into the dimension of faith. They are your commitment to "love" God the way you love to love. It's loving God "with all your heart and with all your soul and with all your mind and with all your strength."[3] Vows are your love gestures to God. They are things that open your heart directly to the mystery of the Person of God.

Yes, there are the specific things God asks us to be involved in, but he allows us to determine the shape our faith takes—how much we pray, whether or not we want to fast and how often, what ministry we want to engage in, how much we want to give, how much time we want to invest in volunteering, what aspect of mission we want to participate in, and so on. Vows help us to decide what that looks like for each of us individually. They are born from the conviction that we need to love God in "extra" ways because he deserves more than he demands. But that doesn't mean we wander into the land of vow-making on our own—the believer doesn't ever do things alone.

A Tad Mystical

Spiritual personhood isn't just you loving God all on your own. Remember that Christianity is the result of God indwelling the human soul. Paul asserted, "Do you not know that your body is a temple of the Holy Spirit, who is in you, whom you have received from God?"[4] God has united himself to humans on the level of "being"—before we ever take action in the world.

This is a little difficult to explain, so bear with me.

Only God can unite himself to another on the level of being. We can only join ourselves with others through interactions such as conversation or by doing some activity together (one sings bass, another tenor, and we *join* together in song) or we have a "meeting of the minds" on a particular subject—this is the human sense of "joining."

When God joins himself to you, however, the things you do proceed from both God and you (assuming your heart is submitted to his presence). A graced action is not a blend of

God operating with you; it is both of you acting together as one—fully human and fully divine. The act belongs to you and it belongs to God. It is God's action and your action at the same time. We are talking about a joining on the level of personhood. God and human are united and act out as persons *together*. This is the mystery of faith.

An action that is a graced self-expression is more than a human action; it is a man or woman's act as a person and God's act as a Person—at the same time, in the same person. For example, you come home from work exhausted. You face your family and God says within your heart, "Smile and take interest!" You feel the inclination to smile (because it is already your own inclination) and you either follow it or sink back into your own tiredness. If you don't engage, the inclination of grace is aborted. But if you do, it is a graced self-expression that is literally human and divine. It is your personal act of self-expression, but you and God are united, expressing one and the same act of love and caring.

To grow in spiritual personhood means you must grow in deeper union with God on a personal level. It means you have to cultivate more awareness of the impulses of God's Person within your heart while becoming less and less resistant to those impulses. It means that when you think of your human "self," you associate less and less with the idea of the isolated human self and more and more of the self that is joined with God. This is how you can say along with Paul, "I no longer live, but Christ lives in me."[5] It isn't that you lose yourself but that you discover your true self in Christ. Jesus Christ is no longer the "other" who speaks to you; his voice becomes your voice as you surrender to him.

Another upside to this understanding is, because we are

connected to the Person of God, vow-making is not to be done *alone*. God knows us better than we know ourselves. If we talk with him about the kinds of vows we want to make, how long they should last, and what the objective of the vow should be, he will help guide us into successful vowing. Vows offer a framework where not only the development of personhood can occur but where earlier stages of spiritual formation are reworked and deepened.

Becoming a spiritual "person" requires general obedience to rule-keeping and the conventional principles of discipleship, but it also goes beyond that domain. Becoming your own spiritual person requires realizing there is a point where you have freedom to choose the kind of life you wish to live. Vowing is sweet because it is choosing with firm intention. Vowing helps make your faith yours; you become your own person in Christ. Vows help you focus and dedicate your life to union with God, mission, relationships, and development of gifts and talents, and they help you do what you feel you should in the face of obstacles, setbacks, and limited opportunity.

Dare to Be Different

Unfortunately, I have seen many groups inside churches and Christian ministries that feel they have everything figured out; hence, everyone must look and act the same way. These are not bad people. In fact, they are often very kind and godly. But you will not see much individual expression among them. They follow a predetermined set of mannerisms that are considered holy and right.

Sadly, we evangelicals tend to be a kind of "cookie-cutter" culture. Hence, what we wear, how we talk, what we like or dislike, how often we pray or read our Bibles or go to church, and what we do or don't do is universalized. It's as if we believe Christianity is some kind of a retread of Eastern mysticism that forces people to forfeit their distinctiveness as they are absorbed into some great cosmic oneness or sameness.

Paul wrote that we are all different, like the parts of the human body, and he challenged each member to dare to be different—not to act and think the exact same way.[6] Yes, we are all supposed to be holy. Yes, we are all supposed to be moral. Yes, we are all supposed to live ethically. Yes, we are all supposed to establish some kind of spiritual rhythm. But we get to live out our faith in the way we are wired: using our different gifts, passions, and personalities.

Some of us may be more fashionable than others, some more conservative, some more edgy. Some of us are given to prayer, others to service. Some of us are quiet, some more rambunctious. Some of us blossom spiritually in silence and solitude, others in worship. Some are tattoo-friendly, others tattoo-phobic. As persons we get to be different.

I think some like sameness because it makes it easier for us to tell who the insiders are. Just as black leather and a Harley-Davidson are the marks of a biker, and tight jeans, western boots, and a huge silver belt buckle are the marks of a cowboy, certain other external attributes are fancied by some Christians as the marks of Christlikeness. Actually, it is easier to make Christianity about the externals and man-made rules. But the downside is, unless you already fit the predetermined collection of personality traits set by the Christian culture to which you belong, you will be pressured to be something you are not. Christianity will feel restrictive and hold little joy for you.

But there is freedom in Christ. If you are going to become a vower, you have to keep in mind that vows are not done to keep up with everyone else or to hit some "same" level of spirituality—they are about you, your individuality, your love for God, your choices. We vow into personhood, not sameness. Like different pianists have their own touch to the music they play, those who choose to vow can take up the tasks of love any way they feel so inclined. We can each commit ourselves to a life with a unique touch in loving. How fun is that?

Vows help us decide life questions such as: Who am I? Where am I going? How do I get there? And we don't allow ourselves to just respond with philosophical or theoretical answers—we take action! We choose what will shape our lives by deciding what it is we do. But it goes even deeper.

Vowing to perform various practices taps our inner freedom to not just choose what we do but to choose who we want to be. We are not just choosing a restaurant to eat at or a career to pursue, we are choosing to grasp the hand of God and enter into the mystery that is at the heart of life—the very journey of being a God-follower, a pilgrim of the eternal. And it begins to define who we are. We are no longer *just* doctors or lawyers or moms or plumbers or seminarians or Starbucks managers—we are the people of God who live in those places with him, and with us comes his kingdom. We salt the world (making it tastier and preserving its good), and we light up the darkness (things just aren't as bad as they would have been had we not shown up). We may not have the kingdom in full bloom as will happen on the last day, but we love what we *do* have and we keep pressing for more. We are his persons, and as so *we matter*. In the eyes of our beholders—those outside of faith—there is something mysterious about us.

Let's talk more about the "mystery" vowing helps us enter.

6. Vowing into Mystery

Everything you are and think and do is permeated with Oneness.

—Apostle Paul[1]

Vow-making is a lot like falling in love and getting married. Boy notices girl; girl notices boy. Their eyes meet. There is a note of interest, maybe even an unspoken hint of excitement. Conversation occurs. Smiles and laughter erupt. They enjoy the rendezvous. There are a few more chance encounters, which prove to be delightful, and they catch themselves looking forward to seeing the other again. They are left wanting *more*. At some point they plan to meet intentionally, to interact again. This is when a relationship starts to bud. You have no relationship with a person unless you do something intentionally that expresses your love for him or her. In doing loving acts you "realize," or make your love real for, that person. This is where the seeds for future vow-making get planted.

Something about the boy-girl relationship mirrors the one we have with God. Somehow God catches your eye (which is in itself a work of grace) in a moment of understanding where you realize God is real and he is reaching out to you. There is a rush of excitement. Conversations occur (your life opens to God).

59

Smiles and laughter erupt (can it be true that you have caught the attention of *God*?). There are numerous encounters, which prove to be delightful (you are invited to a few church services, have some God-conversations with friends, happen into a Bible study, and so on). And you catch yourself looking forward to encounters with God again. You want *more*. At some point you plan to meet intentionally, to make your interaction more habitual. You choose to go to church or Bible study or have some devotional time, on your own, without the prodding of another. This is when your relationship with God starts to bud. There is no relationship with God unless you do something intentionally that expresses your love for him. In doing loving acts you "realize," or make your love "real" to, God. This is not quite "vowing" yet, but this is where the seeds for vowing get planted.

The church is called the "bride of Christ." That's pretty wild when you consider the ramifications of God using the marriage union as a metaphor to express the kind of relationship he is seeking with us. Paul claims that marriage speaks beyond itself; it speaks of "Christ and the church." It turns out that marriage is a parable of faith, which means there are many rich connections that can be made between the marriage vow and the vows you make in your relationship with God. As in marriage, the vows we make to God are both responses to his love for us and expressions of our love for him.

The Call to Mystery

What motivates a man and a woman to enter into something as serious as a marriage vow? Why would they want to vow to share their whole lives together? In speaking of how men and women would be willing to leave their families of origin in order to take the solemn marriage vow, Paul declares, "This is a profound mystery."[2] Vows are rooted in mystery. The whole love enterprise is a journey into mystery. It is mystery because you don't know what opening yourself to that person really means: How will it change me? What am I risking? Will I be happy? Will I get hurt? Am I being foolish or wise? Wagonloads of questions. Scary ones.

When we enter a vow with God, we are stepping into mystery as well. Vows are not about becoming perfect. They are about interacting, sharing, and exposing our lives to Another—to God. In a vowed relationship we get naked, the worst about us is revealed. Vowed relationships are too close to play cover up. Just as marriage brings out what is really in us, so does vowing to God. Whatever selfishness is in you will rise to the surface; you won't be able to cover it.

A few months ago the community in which I serve as a teaching pastor decided to do some corporate fasting in tandem with the Lenten season. We decided to fast corporately at least one meal on Wednesdays. I really don't like to fast—it's bothersome and uncomfortable. And there is nothing "fast" about it; it makes time go slower and makes the day seem more grueling (I think it should be renamed "slowing"). However, fasting has been a frequent practice in my spiritual journey—that's how I really know I don't like it. I *do* love the interaction with God that this practice affords me. I've learned to reinterpret my hunger for Big Macs as a hunger for God. And since I love corporate expressions of faith, I promised—vowed—to participate in the Wednesday fasts during this six-week period. And as I expected, I started to hate Wednesdays. Something in me gets mad at me for making me hurt. So as the hunger dawned, so did other things: grumpiness, a gnawing impatience, an acute awareness of all the injustices present in my life—injustices imposed on me by *anyone* who asked me to do *anything*.

Vow-making keeps us from abandoning commitments from which we would love to justify our retreat. When we are backed into a corner with no place to run, it tends to solicit a reaction deep within us—the selfishness and self-pity that lurk within enter the ring ready for a fight. We are generally not as good as we think we are. We trick ourselves into believing that we are loving, patient people, but we don't *really* know that we are until someone or something inconveniences us, disappoints us, disrupts us, or takes advantage of us. Then we see what's hiding just below the surface in our souls. And most of the time it ain't pretty. But that's what I love about making vows. We commit to doing the things that make the yuck come out.

On the uncharted, unexplored regions on the edges of ancient maps, cartographers used to write "where dragons lie." Sadly, they lie in all of us—particularly in the uncharted, undiscipled regions of our souls. But thank God the "dragons" leave when we move toward him! And God always helps us understand how they got there in the first place, which is the first step in slaying them.

And this was exactly what our community was going after when we decided to participate in the Lenten season. We wanted to do spiritual things that exposed the negative motives, attitudes, and feelings (and all such "dragons") that were in hiding in our souls, though we weren't on a witch hunt. Nor were we fasting so we could *say* we were fasting. Truth be told, we were simply on a quest for a deeper encounter with God.

The point of vow-making is not to *do* what it is we vow to do, nor is the goal of vowing the sense of accomplishment we get as we perform the details of the vow. The point of the whole vowing enterprise is the pursuit for more interaction with God. Vows are to a *Person*, not just to *doing* a thing.

More than Vows

In every wedding ceremony I perform, the couple says something like the following in their vows to each other: "I will honor, respect, and hold your needs before my own. I promise to keep you as my one true love, as God has ordained, for all of my life." And these vows are always said in the context of me asking them, "Do you promise to do this from this day forward, for better, for worse, for richer, for poorer, in sickness and in health, to love and to cherish, till death do you part?"

Of all the weddings I have done in my years of pastoral care, I have never had a bride or a groom say their primary goal was the vow itself. No one comes to the altar thinking, *At last, I found someone who will let me "honor" and "respect" them; someone whose needs I can place above my own. I'm not picky—it could be anyone—I just need to vow!*

Every couple comes to the altar with the dream of sharing their lives with the one they have come to love. They aren't looking for just *anyone* to vow to—in fact, the whole vowing proposition is a bit scary for them. But they push past the scare because they have found someone so wonderful they want to vow to them specifically in order to move into the mystery of sharing life together. They're not sure what that will look like in the future; it, too, is mystery. But the vow is never the point; life with the other person always is—as mysterious and uncertain as that is.

The vows we make to God are also rooted in mystery. In the Daily Office vow I am currently participating in, my goal is not just to have four "mini-devotions" each day as an end in itself. I practice what I have vowed to do, but my focus is not on the doing but on the journeying of my soul through the doing into the mystery that is God. I am trusting that God will touch my life as I journey through vowed practice. As he does, I respond and enter more deeply into God. If I do not hold on to this view, my mini-devotions lack the ground that gives them life. They quickly become tedious. My vow to the Daily Office is a way I can give a faith-response to God. But it is a response to the mystery of what can be realized between myself and God. I am in pursuit of the "otherness" of God himself. So, vows are a way we can enter into the mystical experience of being the bride of Christ.

Couples who fall in love naturally reach for the mystery of entering into a deeper relationship with the one they love through vowing. Their vow is an effort to give that mystery concrete expression. Vows are a specific response to each other—a sign of a couple's desire to love the other without reservation. They are a response to mystery—the mystery of becoming "one" with another person. The same holds true for those of us who are lovers of God. There is something within us that longs to enter a deeper relationship with him—as mystical as that might seem. Our vows are an effort to give that mystery concrete expression. My vow to the Daily Office is a specific response to God—a sign of my desire to love him without reservation. In this sense my vow is not just a human promise that springs from a sense of moral duty or the quest to live out my life in a certain way. It is different from the decision to start dieting or following a budget. I vow in response to mystery—the mystery of moving more into becoming "one" with God.

One could argue that Christ-followers should pursue God and participate in a robust devotional life without ever vowing to do it, and I would have to agree. All this "should" happen and "could" happen in response to the general vow believers make at the point of their conversion. However, on a psychological level of personal realization and conscious determination, it usually doesn't. Ergo, I vow.

Vows Are God-Dates

Gail and I have been married more than thirty years and we still go on dates. There's something about dating that keeps love fresh and active. Technically, married couples shouldn't have to date—we are married. We have near constant interaction through living together, communicating, being physically intimate, and so on. Why would we need to "date"?

We date because dating is about being intentional. Dating puts our love under the microscope—it's a close-up look at why we entered the marriage vow to begin with. Dating converts what sleeps in the domain of *intention*—the "we should" or "we could" thoughts—into purposeful *action*. Dates give concreteness to our love. We date to be together in a heightened, more radical way—more than just the way we are when we walk around the same house. We date to talk in a more intimate way—not just about "stuff" but about feelings and hopes. On my dates with Gail we laugh a lot, cry sometimes, and kiss sometimes. We always hold hands.

Dating is romantic and romance is demanding. There must be planning and effort. And it comes at a cost—not always money, but sacrifice on some level is always involved. The more you plan, the more romance you will have. And the more you work to make the experience near perfect, the more meaningful and wonderful it will be. Dating makes love intentional, and therein lies its power.

On our fifteenth wedding anniversary, I told Gail to pack enough clothes for four days. I arranged everything in advance: the babysitting, the travel arrangements, the hotels, and tickets for the events we were to attend. She knew nothing about my plans.

"Where are we going?" she asked.

"I'm not telling," I responded.

After bludgeoning me with questions for a couple of days, she gave up trying to unearth my secret plan. I knew she was excited, and *not* knowing seemed to provoke anticipation in her. The night before we were to leave I surprised her with the early arrival of the sitter. I told her to grab her stuff—*right now!*—and jump in the car. She smiled and instantly complied.

We traveled for a few hours, stayed in a cozy inn, and got up early the next morning. We then drove about two miles to the train station. She still had no idea where we were headed.

We boarded the Amtrak bound for Illinois and enjoyed a snowy, Dr. Zhivagoesque ride from central Wisconsin to Union Station in Chicago. We then took a cab to a lovely hotel with a fireplace and fifteen red roses waiting. The next four days were filled with preplanned dinners, plays, concerts, and shopping.

Gail had no knowledge of what we were going to do until I told her to get ready. But she so enjoyed the experience. And instead of nagging me daily with questions, she just sat back and experienced the moment. She said it was "romantic."

Vows are powerful because they add romance to our faith. I think about and plan my activities around my vow to the Daily Office—my special moments with God. I have a number of books that talk about it—*The Divine Hours* by Phyllis Tickle, *Celtic Daily Prayer* by the Northumbria Community, and *The Book of Common Prayer* are three great examples—they are like books full of "date-ideas" for me. I am constantly searching for ways to make my mini-devotions meaningful and rich. I've found the more effort I put into every detail of my God-dates, the more wonderful they are. My vow simply makes my love for God intentional. This reminds me of something Isaiah wrote, "Clear the way through the wilderness for the LORD! Make a straight highway through the wasteland for our God! Fill in the valleys, and level the mountains and hills. Straighten the curves, and smooth out the rough places. Then the glory of the LORD will be revealed."[3]

Sounds like a date to me.

Vows Create Stability

Once a couple has shared sufficient experiences, they come to the place where they don't want to be apart; they want to share life together. They want to make their love and interactions permanent. The same holds true in our relationship with God. After we have had sufficient graced-experiences with God, we want to continue in those—we want them to define the love-relationship we have with God and to give our relationship stability and permanence. That requires specific commitment. Vows give us that.

We can only have an abiding relationship of love with another person when we are committed to act toward that person—and to keep acting toward him or her in a certain way. That is what vowing is all about. The kind of commitments we make to one another determines the kind of love-relationship we enter into with him or her.

Just as a couple vows to share more and more of their lives together, we vow to share more and more of our lives with God. Our goal is perfect union of mind, will, and heart. A vow is a gesture toward stabilizing that commitment. We enter vows, not as a way to pursue "interest" about God but rather as a framework to facilitate an ongoing openness to God—where the Spirit of God becomes present in the life of the one vowing.

While God's Spirit is active in the life of every believer (whether one vows or not), vowing is an intentional witness to that activity—it is an open commitment precisely because God's activity is there and one does not want to miss it. Vows are the commitments we make to stay open to God in a certain way, one that causes us to live in the "now-ness" of his grace.

There are at least four specific commitments that help bring the unity couples are after as they declare their marital vows: living together, communicating with each other, conversion to each other's ideals, and physical expression of love. And these four things have counterparts in the vows we make to God. Let's look at those next.

7. MARRIAGE, SEX, AND VOW-MAKING

Go ahead then, do what you promised! Keep your vows!
—*Jer. 44:25*

We're going to talk a lot about marriage in this chapter. You may not be married, but this segment is important to read if you want to understand the wonder of vowing. So if you're single, no skipping on to the next chapter! Marriage is a great metaphor that will give vow-making a little more clarity. So married, single, or eunuch, hang in there, baby.

What motivates a couple to move into something as serious as the marriage vow parallels what motivates us to enter vows with God. Couples who jump into marriage are not after something to do, they are looking for relationship. Marital vows are a reach for relationship—a longing for connection with the other person. A couple vows because they want to bind themselves to the promise of the kind of life and relationship they have enjoyed. The reason the marriage vow is scary is because it limits the couple's freedom and options. But they are willing to take the plunge in order to give their love direction and purpose, as well as staying power.

The Vow

Vows express what each expects from the other in the relationship. Vows always have in view the hope of growing into oneness. Marriage vows give structure to a couple's longing to be together for life, which is no easy enterprise. (It usually isn't until after a couple marries that they begin to grasp how hard "togetherness" really is.) But their vows provide a safe context for the couple to roll up their sleeves and work (sometimes *claw* and *scratch*) through their differences. This helps them grow closer together and prevents them from emotionally drifting away from each other. Hence, the marriage vow is a concrete, intentional, and specific commitment that helps a couple experience the wonder of unity. This is why vows transcend a simple "list" of things we promise to do.

This is the very same reason any of us would make a vow to God (that is, to participate in special prayer emphasis, engage in a season of study, join a period of special fasting, take a vow of chastity before marriage, and so on). We are not just wanting to do something; we want a deeper relationship with God. And just like it is difficult for two human beings to cultivate a growing, deepening love that results in unity, it doesn't take long to discover that loving God with all your heart and mind and soul is not an easy endeavor either. We seem to carry wagonloads of internal resistance to abandoned and surrendered love.

So we make vows to God in order to give our love for him direction, purpose, and staying power—though they limit our freedom and options. In the context of our vows, we are stipulating what our signs of love for God will be—all in the hope of growing into oneness with God himself.

Those who have a negative view of vows (like marriage) are not focused on the mystery of love but only on the actual

70

requirements inherent in the vow—these boys and girls are the technical bean counters, fretting over what and how much they are required to do. But it is unifying love—not fulfilling requirements—that is the deepest desire of a vow, the real goal of a vow.

There are four specific characteristics of marriage that are assumed to be part of the marital vow. These are what enable couples to snag the unity they are after. They include: hanging out together, keeping the lines of communication open with each other, negotiating which ideals they want to embrace as a couple, and the physical expression of their love—their sexuality. We'll see how these four characteristics have relevance to the vows we make to God.

Hanging Out Together

Sharing everyday life together is the only way a couple will ever experience a true union of heart and mind. Life's experiences always shape and challenge who we are as persons, as well as who we are becoming. If you don't have continuous interaction with the one you love in real time, you won't be able to integrate and harmonize your experiences together—you'll end up being like ships passing in the night. You'll grow apart instead of growing together. One of the main reasons the marriage vow is confined to you and one other person is because of the limitations of time and space—you can really only have this kind of intimacy with one other person.

The togetherness of marriage mirrors the way God wanted to make himself accessible to us. He wants to be with us—right in the mix of the contours of everyday life. He loves to engage us within the potentials and flaws of the human experience and within the possibilities and limitations of our fallen world. This is the primary focus of the vows we make to God. Our goal is to do things that help us intentionally recognize the presence of God as we walk through our experiences, insights, and responses of the day. We simply want to hang with God, to do life together with God. Paul exclaimed, "In him we live and move and have our being."[1] Based on this text, the Book of Common Prayer directs us to pray, "Heavenly Father, in you we live and move and have our being: We humbly pray you so to guide and govern us by your Holy Spirit, that in all the cares and occupations of our life we may not forget you, but may remember that we are ever walking in your sight; through Jesus Christ our Lord. Amen."[2]

God wants a day in and day out relationship with his people. Jesus came to earth to open a way for there to be a union of God's life with ours. Grace is God's presence with us in time. Grace brings a new way of living to bear—a new quality of life. This life is not simply added onto what we experience as ordinary. Grace is not like a super-unleaded gasoline pumped into our human tanks so we can function more efficiently. Nor is grace a new layer of existence that covers up the old. Grace is the free and gratuitous communication of God's life into our human experience—God wants to hang with us. It creates new birth and new creation in the context of real time. And it results in giving us full utilization and meaning for human life. This is God and humankind uniting—us living together in what becomes sacred space. This is a divine-human interaction, a relationship of cooperation. This is why we do radical things like vow-making—we don't want this grace to be forgotten or ignored as far as we are concerned.

I vowed to my wife, Gail, to stay in her presence. The same goes here. The psalmist wrote, "As for me, it is good to be near God. I have made the Sovereign LORD my refuge."[3] When God told Moses to lead the Israelites into the wilderness, Moses answered, "If your Presence does not go with us, do not send us up from here."[4]

Being with God should be our focus of the vows we make. The psalmist said, "My whole being follows hard after You and clings closely to You."[5] That needs to be a snapshot of the motive behind entering a vowed season for prayer, ministry, or spiritual growth. We need to be like Moses and say, "If your Presence does not go with us, we can't go anywhere near this whole 'vowing' thing."

As marriage includes another, vow-making to God includes him—he is actually present in the mix. We are then captured by a transcendent, bigger-than-us, otherly experience with the living God. It is precisely this otherliness, this transcendent connection, that makes vow-making so rich.

Communication

Communication is the circulatory system of any marriage—it gives it life. If two people don't talk frequently enough or deeply enough, they never experience true unity and oneness of heart. But communication is not an easy thing to do. Men and women tend to misunderstand each other. We misread each other. We even misjudge each other. If we are serious about communicating, we must commit to breaking through the barriers of misunderstanding. However, the temptation is to let things slide—to stop negotiating through the "he said-she said" dialectic. But yielding to ease in the arena of communication would be a violation of the marital vow. If we refuse to continue talking openly and deeply, we reject each other as persons. This is why communication needs to remain the number-one priority in your marriage. The fact is, the commitment to not shut down emotionally and to keep communicating with each other in an open-hearted way is even more important than the physical dimension of sex in marriage.

Communication is critical in our relationship with God as well. All vows involving faith need to be chock-full of communication. Vows are unintelligible without an accompanying commitment to communicate with God about what it is you are doing. You need to talk with God about the vows you want to enter. Even if the vow is specifically a vow to pray, you have to pray about praying—you need to talk with God about how you are feeling and what you are expecting as you participate in a vow. Listen too. You may feel a sense that this is not a good time to enter a vow or that it should involve something other than you considered. If you learn to grow still and listen, you will sometimes hear God's voice—not always in words, but you will have a sense whether you are on track or not.

Talk with God as you practice your vow. If you have vowed to fast, talk with God about what is going on in your head and the way the fast is impacting your soul—even if it is a horrible experience. It is this kind of communication that ushers life into your relationship with God. It is more the point of the vow than implementing the specifics of the vow could ever be. Remember, God is not after human performance; he wants access to your heart. As you share openly, there is a growth in knowledge and love between you and God.

Negotiation

The attempt to move together into oneness in marriage is a cool idea that carries a bunch of "scary" with it. It's cool when you discover you share similar attitudes and values and you bask in the warmth of agreement. But it gets scary and just plain awful when you run into things you clash over, revealing that the two of you are complete opposites. There are lots of good reasons for the differences: you both come from a different family of origin; you both have a unique personality and set of interests and passions; and most significant of all, one of you is male and the other female (our psychological and physiological differences are so profound, I sometimes wonder if the whole call to "oneness" isn't some kind of cosmic tease). One of the most popular marriage books in recent years is titled *Men Are from Mars, Women Are from Venus*. On some level, your marriage partner will always seem like a bit of an alien to you. Men and women are definitely different.

To hit anything close to "unity" when couples house such differences, they must commit to finding common ground— to discovering mutual goals and ideals they both can buy into. This means they must learn to negotiate—to know when to give in and when to ask the other person to give in. But this must be done with wisdom and without any kind of coercion. When differences become apparent, the couple needs to take time to assess which of their two positions is the most wise or admirable. (It helps to get some counsel from godly friends and family.) Then they must choose to move toward the view that represents what they both believe to be the best and highest ideal. Obviously, doing this takes guts and sacrifice; your position may not be the one chosen. This is risky, and sometimes painful business. Our natural impulse is to fight for our own positions no matter what—even if we know deep inside that we may be wrong. But negotiating into common ground (as awful as it feels) is a wonderful experience.

Vow-making to God is also both wonderful and awful. Loving God carries both invitation and threat. At times you discover you hold similar attitudes and values (though not nearly as clearly or purely as God does), and there are other times, perhaps the majority of the time, when you realize you are complete opposites and clash. God warns, "'For my thoughts are not your thoughts, neither are your ways my ways,' declares the LORD."[6]

There are a boatload of reasons for the differences: he is God, you are not; he is holy, you are not . . . enough said. On a number of levels God will simply not make sense to you: "Oh, the depth of the riches of the wisdom and knowledge of God! How unsearchable his judgments, and his paths beyond tracing out! Who has known the mind of the Lord? Or who has been his counselor?" is how Paul put it.[7]

Because we enter the journey of faith declaring Jesus as Lord, we have already committed to the notion that his ideals and values should win out over ours. He is our God, and we need to remain open to any change he desires. The vow-making gesture is our commitment and decision in advance to conform to his way whenever we hit a issue on which we are not in agreement. As his followers we pledge ourselves to a continual conversion of our attitudes and values in a pursuit to bring them into conformity with his own. Go God.

Physical Expression

Marriage is a potpourri of loves: friendship, devotion, rational or intellectual love, sacrifice, and so on. But the love that is peculiar to this human bond is physical love. The Greek word for human physical love is *eros*. We get our English word "erotic" from it. *Eros* is the physical expression of the love between a husband and a wife, and there is something about it that reflects our relationship with God.

Talking about sexuality and God in the same context definitely makes most people feel uncomfortable. Perhaps the uneasiness comes from the way sexuality is abused in our culture and thereby loses its sanctity. Or perhaps it is because we have hints of ancient Gnosticism in us, which held that all that is physical is evil, and comparing our spiritual relationship with Christ with the sheer physicality of the sexual relationship seems a little out-there. But the correlation is clearly put forth in the biblical text (read Song of Solomon, Paul's teaching on marriage, and so on).

The Importance of Eros

My brother, Mark, runs an organization called Laugh Your Way to a Better Marriage. He conducts marriage seminars in churches and corporations and works directly with the

Pentagon to bring marriage enrichment to our troops. He helps a lot of marriages. He loves to tell stories of estranged couples who hardly sit next to each other at the start of his events and end up cuddling and holding hands by the end. He claims that physicality, touch, goo-goo eyeing, teasing whispers, and good sex are all crucial to a healthy marriage relationship.

Of course, physicality is only one dimension. There is the need for friendship, the promise of faithfulness, a demonstrated commitment, and the basic chemistry of physical attraction for carnal love to be fulfilling. But sexual love is crucial to a marriage; and proves to be a kind of "cleansing" for the relationship.

A sexless marriage is a dead marriage. Why? Two reasons: First, because all the other forms of love are not unique to marriage, they are also shared with others outside the marriage bond. For example, you can be friends with many people. Similarly, you can generally be a faithful and devoted person to whomever you know. Attraction isn't even unique—many different people may appear attractive to you.

Sexual love, by contrast, is exclusive to marriage—at least that is God's intent. Physical love was designed by God to be shared by one man, one woman, together, for life. To exclude carnal love from a marriage is to domesticate it, to make the relationship common—the marital bond ends up looking like something one could share with a coworker or a friend.

The second reason a sexless marriage isn't a legitimate marriage is because of the "otherliness" of sex. Sexual love cannot be shared between two people unless they are both present. Fantasy can be shared separately, but fantasy isn't real. Real sexual love is shared love; it is "otherly." It demands the participation of another. With physical love you go out of yourself in a trajectory of ecstasy—to a place where you cease to be in control of yourself. You become completely vulnerable, open, engaged, and yielded to each other. In this ecstasy you lose yourself to your partner in a way you would never dare in any other setting. And it culminates in an experience that the Bible says is "as strong as death."[8] Theologians have suggested that because there is a total giving of the self in the sexual act, it is a kind of "little death."[9]

Sexual love should come packed with devotion, but it is more than devotion. You can be devoted to a job or your softball team. Sexual love should be accompanied by wagonloads of friendship, but it is more than friendship. Sexual love should have intrinsic respect, but it is more than respect. You respect your parents. The uniqueness of physical love is what makes marriage, marriage.

The implications of comparing human lovers with the divine relationship are many. If one accepts that this comparison and symbolism are valid, there are many parallels to be made: the "mystery" of attraction, the power of the emotion, the openness (nakedness) and ecstasy, the natural ebb and flow of physical interest in relationships, the flirting and playfulness, and so on. Often it is *eros* that initially fuels the love interest between a man and a woman—it is our first love. It is the moving power of pursuit, and by analogy, it represents the moving force of our faith expression. If a sexless marriage is dead, a passionless faith is dead too.

So how does physical love relate to the vows we make to God? In a number of ways:

1. Vows speak of exclusivity. *Eros* love is privileged love. In this kind of love there is a desire for the couple to be emotionally and physically separate from others. In friendship love, if a person wanted you to be their only friend and no one else's—that would be a red flag. We should have many friends. But not in romance. Romantic love is exclusive love. Only two should be in on this—that defines normal.

The first commandment in the decalogue carries the idea of exclusivity: "You shall have no other gods."[10] God wants to be ours and wants us to be his. It is because he is God Almighty that he can pull off being "only" with me and "only" with you at the same time. No dissolution, no infidelity on his part. But we cannot. We must carefully watch what we allow our attention and love to be attached to. James warns, "You're cheating on God. If all you want is your own way, flirting with the world every chance you get, you end up enemies of God and his way. And do you suppose God doesn't care? "The proverb has it that 'he's a fiercely jealous lover.'"[11] God gets jealous of our love for other things. He wants exclusivity. Our specific vows to God give concreteness to the idea that we are going to live in a way that expresses we belong to God *alone*.

2. Vows are a kind of flirting. To flirt is to chase another. Happy couples do this all the time. Gail and I have been dating for over thirty-two years, and we still flirt. You can hear it in the tone of our voices as we talk with each other; it's in the love names we call each other; it's in the passing touch; it's present in the lingering stare from across the room; it's in those teasing whispers—flirting adds joy and playfulness to human sexuality. I usually call Gail several times a day and will often open with something like, "Is this the most beautiful girl in the world?" To which she'll reply, "Maybe."

Flirting. Flirting is all about "the chase."

Does God flirt with us? I think so. In the 1800s Francis Thompson referred to God as "the Holy Hound of Heaven."[12] The imagery familiar in Thompson's day of a bloodhound on a dashing hunt to track a scent powerfully reflects how God tracks us down the corridors of our lives to capture us with his relentless love. The psalmist penned, "Is there anyplace I can go to avoid your Spirit? . . . If I climb to the sky, you're there! If I go underground, you're there! If I flew on morning's wings to the far western horizon, you'd find me in a minute—you're already there waiting!"[13]

God chases us. And he shows no pause or caution in it.

Think of all the times in your life when something happened or was said and it just seemed too coincidental—you suspected God was in it. Those moments are like winks from God to us, nudges of love. He flirts. Then there are the ways God speaks of us: "I have summoned you by name; you are mine."[14] *You are mine*, he says. How cool is that? The prophet Zephaniah said, "[God] will take great delight in you, he will quiet you with his love, he will rejoice over you with singing."[15] He delights in us and sings over us. Sounds flirty to me.

I think vow-making is one of the ways we can chase God in return. The psalmist said, "Seven times a day I praise you."[16] He was chasing! I see my vow to the Daily Office as a daily pursuit of God. Last year our faith community entered a thirty-day vow to experiment with the various classic disciplines and how they might impact our spirituality. We planned times of silence, solitude, fasting, worship, and so on. It was a wonderful experience. But what made it so was we saw it as a chase for God—not as a spiritual competition or quest for perfection.

Chasing after God is sweet. Even a peppering of simple one-sentence prayers throughout your day, like "I love you, Jesus" or "I think you are amazing and so generous" or "Praise to you, God—I belong to you" or singing a simple praise chorus, are all good examples of spiritual flirting. You are simply chasing after him. You are flirting. And flirting adds joy and playfulness to spirituality.

3. Vows foster passion. In the marriage bond, the man and woman both want to be adored—to have someone long for them with "blazing fire."[17] Fire is a great metaphor because it is both fascinating and dangerous. Just sit by a blazing campfire and try to look elsewhere. It's too fascinating to ignore. Fire is also dangerous because it consumes and controls what it possesses. Passion does that. We want passion from our mates. We want them to be fascinated about us, and we want it to consume them, to control them. We also want to feel that way about them in return.

The fire that burns in romantic love is a reflection of the kind of passion we need to cultivate in our relationship with God. He certainly is passionate about us—passionate enough to focus his attention on us night and day. He was passionate enough to go to a cross—he was consumed by his love for us.

We should be on fire for God. Passionate. We are told to "never be lacking in zeal, but keep your spiritual fervor, serving the Lord."[18] Remember the "devotion" texts: "Devote yourselves to prayer, being watchful and thankful."[19] And, "Be careful to devote themselves to doing what is good."[20] In Chapter 1 we showed how the word "devote" is derived from the word "to vow." Vowing gives expression to passionate devotion—devotion that is explicit and unambiguous.

4. Vows create anticipation. When physical love is dawning, a couple is filled with anticipation. There will be touch; there will be contact; there will be connection. This is no longer flirting; this is the real deal. Exclusivity, passion, and flirting are already part of this fabric. But it is time to actually touch—physically.

God anticipates our presence. The psalmist paints a picture of God always standing by, watching to see whether or not we are interested in him. He knows "when I sit" and "when I rise." He perceives "my thoughts from afar" and discerns "my going out and my lying down." He is "familiar with all my ways."[21]

When I was in high school, I usually met each morning before school with other believers for a short time of prayer. One particular day I was running behind. I got up late, missed the morning prayer meeting, took a couple of tests, and didn't even think of praying until lunch time. It was just after noon when I was walking down the hall and said under my breath, "I love you, Lord." I kid you not—I heard in my heart, "Good morning!" I remember being surprised and then having the distinct impression that he had been waiting to connect with me all day. *Anticipation.*

Jesus said, "Here I am! I stand at the door and knock. If anyone hears my voice and opens the door, I will come in."[22] He is present. He is ready to engage. He waits for us to answer.

Vowing fuels anticipation in our souls with our pre-decisions to pull away into private places in order to linger and wait for God in the vowed practice. Vows anticipate God's touch. In reaching out to God through our vows, we wait on God—for him to speak into our lives and into our world.

Some years ago I participated in a vowed forty-day fast. Though the fast involved not eating for forty days, the goal was not the act of fasting; it was to create space in which God could enter. The psalmist penned, "Be still before the LORD and wait patiently for him."[23] This is the only valid goal for vow-making. And it takes patience because we have to work through distractions. Just like a couple needs to fight to get alone and allow passion to build, you and I must fight through distraction in the pursuit of God.

Distraction is normal, but must be overcome. When distraction comes, turn from it to look for God. This is spiritual purification. It is letting go and unloading anything that distracts you from your Lover. We are the ones who make room for God—we must anticipate him.

5. *Vows bring us together.* The Bible uses physical union as an example of the way God works in us. It does not do so to make us feel awkward. It is often pointed out that Jonah's time in the belly of the fish foreshadows Jesus's time in the tomb—but no one is suggesting Jesus was in an actual fish when they make the comparison. The analogy is just an analogy for illumination. That is what is happening here. The analogy of physical love gives us illumination into the divine-human connection—no one is suggesting the connection is in any way sexual.

Touch is a very powerful thing—especially when sexuality is rumored. As kissing and caressing proceed, the senses are heightened, desire rises, and the couple begins to get lost in the moment. They become lost in each other.

This pattern is true of deep spiritual moments as well. We begin with a yearning to connect. We belong to God exclusively; we have flirted with the hope of this moment to be alone; and we anticipate his coming with our faith. Now we stretch out to touch him with our hearts. The Bible calls this worship. This often gets very physical: sometimes we kneel, lie face down, lift our hands, cover our faces, cry, lift our voices in song, or utter prayers—we are reaching out to touch him. We love him.

At some point, as you linger, you come to a place where God begins to supernaturally illumine your soul with divine light—he touches back. You become aware of his real presence. There is an actual structural change of consciousness. You feel him. You sense his touch. Sometimes it seems you hear him whisper, but often there are no words—just images. Or his presence seems to deeply impact you in a moment of intimacy. You find yourself drinking his presence in, like the bride in the song who says, "Let him kiss me with the kisses of his mouth— for your love is more delightful than wine."[24]

There is nothing quite as "exposing" as human sexuality. A couple enters a marital vow as an act of trust in the shared love they have already experienced and known. It is in this context that they feel safe enough to be open, naked, and vulnerable with each other, and they are willing to give themselves to each other both emotionally and physically. The marriage vows only have merit in the context of a sense at the core of a couple's being that they are wildly and radically loved.

In the same way, believers enter the arena of vow-making as an act of trust in the love we have already experienced and known from God. And it is in this context that we feel "safe" enough to vow—to open ourselves up to the love, mercy, and scrutiny of God—to be open, "naked," and vulnerable before him. Here we are willing to give ourselves to God in complete trust—we let him touch the secret and hidden places in our lives to bring cleansing and healing. Vows only have merit when we know at the core of our being that God wildly and unconditionally loves us.

Vows are a promise to be open to the wonder of God but not mysteriously or ambiguously. Vows are the promise to be open to the mystery of God through some very concrete choices and decisions. We choose to give ourselves completely to God. The idea of *eros* in vow-making goes to the point that we don't vow in order to become perfect or to establish consistency in our faith walk. We vow to the person of God. We vow to intimacy—to know and be known—to be "naked," as it were, before him. This is a place of union with God. This is physicality. This is interaction. This is touch. This is coming together.

The Bible is full of examples of God "coming to" people. When he did, they were changed. God came to King Saul, and he was "changed into a different person."[25] When God came to Peter, the one who had denied Jesus three times in the Gospels, he became a bold preacher for Jesus.[26] The essence of Christianity is God coming to humankind and changing us from the inside—giving us the desire and the motivation to pursue holy things. This working within is what makes Christianity unique from all the religions of the world. We are not Christians like Buddhists are Buddhists. We are not Christians like Hindus are Hindus. We don't just choose to be Christians—it is a work of God within us, a result of his stirring.

When God stirs within us, it produces new motivations within us. Motivations are the things that move people to action. Most people in our culture are motivated by covetousness or greed (resulting in the pursuit of wealth or possessions), by ambition (resulting in the pursuit of status, position, or power), or by lust (resulting in the pursuit of sensual delights from food to sex). If there were no motivations in the human life, there would be no pursuits.

Motivations cause us to spring to action. Christianity is all about God creating *new* motivations within the human heart—stirring us, giving us desire. David wrote, "Delight yourself in the LORD and he will give you the desires of your heart."[27] Paul asserts that God is the one who "works" in us to cause us "to will and to act" the way he wants us to.[28] And as a result we become zealous of good works.[29]

Divine stirring produces in us a desire to engage with God. Biblical metaphors like "fighting the good fight," "pressing toward the mark," "running the race," and so on, are all snapshots of what God's stirring makes us look like. It is this working that enables us to actually change when we hear preaching or teaching or when we study doctrine.

These holy stirrings abort motivations like greed, ambition, and lust, and they replace them with motivations like holy fear (we care about how our actions impact God and others), hope (an affection that reaches into heaven for what God will do in our lives), love (deep affection for God and others), joy (an expectation that good is being worked into our lives), sorrow (a broken admission of our desperate need for God), hatred (for sin and evil), thanksgiving (a recognition that everything good comes from God), compassion (being touched by what touches others), and zeal (a fervency to do good).

When the divine moves in our interior life and will, we experience a kind of spiritual marriage. This is where our love for God begins to move beyond the intellect and our souls begin to share in divine life. There is a coming together. This is the real reason why we enter the arena of vow-making.

Remember, we don't enter vows in an attempt to be perfect. Vows are only appropriate when there is nothing in this world that would justify doing them but love for God alone. We don't vow to be "better Christians" or to attain perfection; we don't vow to get God to love us more; we don't vow to get ourselves to do what we don't seem to be able to do but want to do. The value of vowing lies precisely in the fact that nothing could justify it except our love for the person of God and the kind of life he offers us in Jesus Christ. We vow into that.

8. THE PROBLEM OF THE WILL

I can do all things through Christ who strengthens me.
—Apostle Paul[1]

I really want to live right. I want to love and be loved. I want to like and be liked. I want to be transparent, giving, selfless, kind, gentle, full of the fruit of the Holy Spirit—the whole deal. I think all of us do. And truth is, I have my moments. After times of abandon in his presence in prayer, study, meditation, or reflection, I carry a fragrance, a palpable weight that steadies my soul and makes me bigger than I am.

But when the glory of my devotional moments begins to fade and I enter the rough-and-tumble of my day, I find deep within myself a piece that is partly fraud and poisoned with deceit. Bummer. Something in me still loves selfishness and wants to maneuver situations to my own advantage. I don't like that self-centeredness is there, and I love to pretend that it isn't. But it is. And because this dualism *is* in me, I flip-flop. Sometimes I live for God; sometimes I don't.

It's reminiscent of the jingle from the famous Hershey's

candy bar commercial for Mounds and Almond Joy (you'll remember it if you're over thirty): "Sometimes you feel like a nut. Sometimes you don't." Sometimes I feel like being nice; sometimes I don't. Sometimes I feel like forgiving; sometimes I don't. And so on. It's like the "want to" in my soul is fickle and wobbly. I hate it. But that's me. And I think most of us can relate. If we were honest with ourselves, most of us would have to admit that we are less consistent than we should be or want to be. It's a problem of will; somewhere it went bad. However, vow-making proves to be very beneficial when dealing with our wills.

Back to the Beginning

At the risk of sounding overly simplistic, here is a short version of the Bible: Reality as we know it is the result of a God who created everything we see. Yet, he is not limited by what he made—he lives both inside (he is immanent) and outside (he is transcendent) of creation. He created the world because he wanted to be a part of it—to flood his life into it. As part of a means to this end, he created a race of beings that would be able to represent his wisdom and care within creation—to be his vicars. And he created them to be a little different than everything else here, to be bearers of something unique. He gave us a *will*.

In the Genesis narrative God creates, God sustains, and God invites humans to participate in developing creation by tending the Garden[2] and naming the animals.[3] We were called to care for creation *with* him. No doubt, in this co-rule nexus we occupy the smallest role, but it is a critical one! Scripture claims he breathed into us (not into any other creature) his very breath.[4] His breath in the human life was the chief way God was entering his creation. He wanted his glory to be present in this world through the human experience and human choice. God told Adam and Eve what was right and what was wrong. They simply obeyed. Their wills were aligned with God's purposes. This is how God's kingdom was to be established in the earth.

But in tragic irony the very beings God created in order for him to have access into the world rebelled against his intention. We lost our way. It was the great theologian Augustine (from way back in the fourth century) who first took the position that the fall of humanity was all about our "choosing"—the human will. He held that God gave humans wills so we could represent God's right and wrong in creation. Using the power of the will, God intended that human beings co-rule creation with God now and throughout eternity. But in an act of rebellion (a perversion of the will), Augustine claimed the human will was "bent" (Lat. *incurvatus*). This made the human will do something it was never designed to do. It stopped obeying God's right and wrong and started instead to determine right and wrong all on its own. This is the dawning of disobedience—or the will gone wild.

Remember, God initially put a "will" inside human beings for the purpose of giving us the capacity to choose to do what he called "good" and to oppose what he called "evil." What happened in the Fall was that the will became *self-moving*. Let me explain.

The Dysfunctional Will

I like the cruise control in my car. I get up to cruising speed, hit the "on" button, push "set," and I'm on my way until I hit the brake or turn the thing off. I can cruise for miles and miles on the highway without paying attention to the speedometer, while enjoying the comfort of being able to adjust and readjust my legs and feet. *Nice.* But sometimes there are problems.

I remember one of the first vehicles I had with cruise control. I loved the feature, but the control had a mind of its own. I would get up to cruising speed and hit "set," but it would keep accelerating. It was as if it were *alive.* Cruise controls are not supposed to act independently—they are designed to represent the driver, which, in this case, was me. Cruise control with a mind of its own is dangerous.

Similarly, God gave human beings a will, or the ability to "want to," as a kind of cruise control for the soul. We are to get our marching orders—our sense of right and wrong—from God and then set our lives in motion in that direction by using the power of our will. But somewhere along the way our cruise control got a mind of its own. This changed *everything.*

i, Robot, starring Will Smith, appeared on the big screen in the summer of 2004. The movie is set in Earth-future (AD 2035) where robots are common assistants and workers for their human owners. Though these robots were created never to hurt human beings, something went awry. Somehow these robots uncovered their own "I"—they became self-choosing, self-moving robots, and they went crazy and started killing humans. Though they were created to serve humanity, they chose to use their intellectual powers against their creator. In a way, it's representative of the biblical story of the Fall.

Those of you familiar with Christian catechism remember the great archangel Lucifer, who later becomes "the Satan." If there is anything that captures the essence of how he became a devil, it is a self-moving will. The pronoun "I" took on new meaning when he tried to overthrow God:

"'I will raise my throne above the stars of God, and I will sit on the mount of assembly in the recesses of the north. I will ascend above the heights of the clouds; I will make myself like the Most High.' Nevertheless you will be thrust down to Sheol, to the recesses of the pit."[5]

God never designed the will to be self-moving—it was always to be connected to obedience. The human will was to be used by us to set God's will into motion in the world in order to establish his reign. But we chose to use our wills just to use them—as a kind of power for its own sake, not to represent God. We used it just because we *could*. We wanted without that "want" being connected to something higher than feral desire. We became naughty. This is the fruit of the Fall—the will gone perverse, self-moving, like a muscle tick.

In the first church I pastored, there was a young boy who kept sneaking around and pulling the fire alarms in the church hallways. It took us several visits from the fire department before we caught the little fella. Why did he do it? He was just being naughty. No real reason. He did it just for the giggle of it. He believed that pulling fire alarms was something we do because we *can*. He didn't understand that fire alarms are ordered to a specific purpose—they should only be pulled to warn of a fire. The same holds true for why God gave us the ability to choose in the first place. We were not to choose because we could; our capacity to choose needed to be ordered to something else—to God's will.

The "Wick"ed Will

Augustine claimed the fall of the human race chiefly "bent" (*incurvatus*) the human will into a self-moving will, debilitating our capacity for doing good. A will that is *incurvatus* is morally evil—it cannot behave rightly; it cannot love appropriately. In order to be virtuous and holy, the Christian must be able to love God supremely and other things rightly. Loving rightly is living rightly, which God gave us the ability to do in the Garden, and is that which we lost vis-à-vis the contorted will.

After the Fall, the will was no longer submitted to or ordered to anything outside itself. It became a force unto itself. When human will was dislodged from a greater purpose, it was free to want whatever it wished. Selfishness was born. At one point in *The Confessions* Augustine calls the fallen human will "monstrous"—stretched out of its proper proportion.[6] The problem of the human soul, then, is neither ignorance nor our desire for evil things; the problem is the aberrant human will. Our wills are bent; they became wicked—the word "wicked" means *twisted*, like the wick-ed wood of wicker furniture. This is the root of our disconnection from the Creator.

The good news is God is not just a Creator, but he is also a Redeemer, a Restorer. God found a completely appropriate way to resolve the problem by reconnecting with the human race in order to bring his original dream for us to pass. Jesus Christ came to this planet (entered the limitations of creation) to take on our spiritual death, and he found a way to restore the corrupted human will—a way for our self-moving wills to come again under the reign of God. But before we deal with the divine solution, let's take a quick peek at the human one.

The Land of Trying Harder

There is something in us that believes we could pull off "better" if we just try a little harder. Remember that the lie at the heart of the Fall was that human beings could make it without God—that if they tried hard enough, they could be perfect. Our enemy, Satan, wants us to believe that lie, too—that we can all be better, even perfect, if we just try hard enough, long enough, and consistently enough.

But if you have ever set out on a path of spiritual self-improvement, you soon discover that something is very wrong. No matter how hard you try to stir up your willpower, eventually your will goes AWOL and you end up in sin. Why? One writer cites the reason: "Lord I see it now! Not only what I have done is wrong; I am wrong!"[7]

I remember how excited I was after I came to Jesus. I wanted to please him in every way. I was eager to learn all I could about how to walk with God. I quickly began discovering my "responsibilities" in God. He wanted me to pray, witness, study, go to church . . . and at first, I could keep up with it. But the commands kept coming and the expectations kept rising.

Soon I found I couldn't keep all the plates spinning, and I started to break them. I panicked. I tried to cover up my failure by promising to do better. I didn't believe the Christian life was supernatural—beyond human ability. I thought I should be able to get the Christian life down pat if I just tried a little harder, if I just became more committed. But no matter what I did, I kept crashing. The human solution to the fickle will is to try harder; the divine solution is to surrender—to experience a spiritual breaking of the will.

The Power of Lordship

When Paul makes the claim, "I do not understand what I do. For what I want to do I do not do, but what I hate I do,"[7] he is underscoring the fact that the human will is bankrupt and perverse. The result is we are lost. Our condition is captured in Paul's words, "As it is written: 'There is no one righteous, not even one; there is no one who understands, no one who seeks God. All have turned away, they have together become worthless; there is no one who does good, not even one.'"[8] Not a pretty picture.

The good news is that Jesus came to redeem us. What is interesting is how he does it. The writer of Hebrews claims, "Therefore, when Christ came into the world, he said: 'Sacrifice and offering you did not desire, but a body you prepared for me; with burnt offerings and sin offerings you were not pleased.' Then I said, 'Here I am—it is written about me in the scroll—I have come *to do your will*, O God.'"[9]

Jesus opened the path for making things right between God and humanity by rescuing our will. Adam used the human will wrongly, which spun sin into the human race. Jesus Christ came to use the will rightly, which spun the possibility of righteousness into the human race. This is why Scripture says, "Here it is in a nutshell: Just as [Adam] did it wrong and got us in all this trouble with sin and death, [Christ] did it right and got us out of it. But more than just getting us out of trouble, he got us into life! One man said no to God and put many people in the wrong; one man said yes to God and put many in the right."[10]

Jesus's 911 mission to rescue the human will is seen no more clearly than in the Garden of Gethsemane as he begins his journey to the cross: "Then he said to them, 'My soul is overwhelmed with sorrow to the point of death. Stay here and keep watch with me.' Going a little farther, he fell with his face to the ground and prayed, 'My Father, if it is possible, may this cup be taken from me. Yet *not as I will, but as you will.*'"[11]

Jesus is redeeming the will here—restoring its purpose, putting it back into right order. Here Christ takes the human will (which he had by virtue of being a human being) and uses it to love God supremely and other things rightly. And because he technically represents the whole human race in his actions (he is the federal head of the human race and is referred to as the second Adam[12]), whatever he accomplishes, he accomplishes for us. Jesus finds a way to restore the function of the human will to its original purpose—so you and I can respond to our call to let God be God in us, to surrender our wills from self-moving domination into grateful surrender. This is why God became human: to show us how to live, how to fulfill our destiny as lovers of God and of each other. Now we can find our way back to authenticity (becoming the *imago Dei*—the image of God) not by imitation, but by association—by connecting with the work of Christ through faith.

However, Christ's work does not result in each person's will being fixed so we can now do whatever we want with our wills. No. The way we experience the redemption of the human will is by associating with the person Jesus Christ and *his* redeemed will. Our wills are not fixable—at least not this side of heaven. The way we associate with Jesus and his redeemed will is by declaring Jesus as Lord.

Something transformational happens when we dare to submit to the lordship of Christ. Paul writes, "If you confess with your mouth, 'Jesus is Lord,' and believe in your heart that God raised him from the dead, you will be saved."[13] How wild that salvation is wrapped up in what you do with your will. Declaring the lordship of Christ is a trip to the cross for our aberrant, misbehaved will. Repentance is all about your will bowing in submission and surrender, the place where it is no longer self-moving. Repentance is dying to the impulse to take charge of your life. This is what must be done to your perverted, *incuratus* will. It must be "crucified." You must, in a sense, die. Paul writes, "I have been put up on the cross to die with Christ. I no longer live. Christ lives in me. The life I now live in this body, I live by putting my trust in the Son of God. He was the One Who loved me and gave Himself for me."[14]

But this is not a place where we can go alone. Repentance requires our cooperation, but more than that—it is a gift and a grace.[15] In order to submit to the lordship of Jesus, the *incurvatus* will need to be broken, which requires a peppering of grace. Paul said, "No one can say, 'Jesus is Lord,' except by the Holy Spirit."[16] There needs to be direct action from the Holy Spirit for lordship to happen. In a way, we need to have our perverse wills "mugged."

Mugging Stories

At one time the great Apostle Paul (then called Saul) was dead set against the church—he worked overtime to persecute her members. But God mugged him:

Meanwhile, Saul was still breathing out murderous threats against the Lord's disciples. He went to the high priest and asked him for letters to the synagogues in Damascus, so that if he found any there who belonged to the Way, whether men or women, he might take them as prisoners to Jerusalem. As he neared Damascus on his journey, suddenly a light from heaven flashed around him. He fell to the ground and heard a voice say to him, "Saul, Saul, why do you persecute me?"

"Who are you, Lord?" Saul asked.

"I am Jesus, whom you are persecuting," he replied. "Now get up and go into the city, and you will be told what you must do."[17]

Every follower of Jesus has a mugging story. All of us understand the moment when we became broken and undone—recognizing that there was nothing we could do to save ourselves but surrender to the person of Christ. The goal of God's muggings is captured in a song from the Psalms: "The sacrifices of God are a broken spirit; a broken and contrite heart, O God, you will not despise."[18] A "broken and contrite heart" refers to a breaking of the corrupted will. This is the result of declaring "Jesus is Lord," and it is a powerful thing. Because Jesus recaptured the human will, he became the source of our salvation. Now obedience is within our grasp! We can obey by leaning on Christ and his redeemed will—we live by faith in him. Scripture records, "Although he was a son, he learned obedience from what he suffered and, once made perfect, he became the source of eternal salvation for all who obey him."[19]

Our wills are corrupted, but his will emerges in us as a grace. Paul writes, "He is working in you. God is helping you obey Him. God is doing what He wants done in you."[20] Faith and discipleship were never supposed to be about us committing to *do good* using our own flawed willpower; it was to be about committing to *Christ*—the One who does good things in us vis-à-vis his redeemed will.

In facing the lordship of Christ and the breaking of our hearts and wills, we are positioned to love rightly again. Vowing has this in view. It is a motion of commitment toward brokenness and fresh openness to God in order to love and live appropriately. Vow-making helps to keep the lordship of Christ central in our daily lives and helps us to obey God more consistently.

Let's see *how* and *why* next.

9. WHY VOWS TRANSFORM

I will fulfill my vows to the LORD.
Ps. 116:14

Scripture is clear: God is our Father. We are his sons and daughters. We are the chosen, his sent ones. He believes in us; he trusts us; he calls upon us to represent him. You and I matter. He isn't kidding about destiny. He consistently asks us to be part of his salvation history. We are called to a purpose. The Bible applauds a guy who "served God's purpose in his own genertion" before he died.[1] That's what God wants all of us to do. That's why we are here.

But living a life that matters requires more than just opening one's life to the forgiveness God affords us in Jesus Christ. It requires a lifestyle of perseverance, diligence, persistence, absolute commitment, and even a willingness to die for our faith—which makes having an *incurvatus* will (described in Chapter 8) especially disconcerting. Learning to consistently live under the influence of grace doesn't make God love us more, but it does determine whether or not we fulfill our destiny—the reason we were created to live on this planet. Participating in the mission of God on earth is not mandatory, but it is costly.

If you were to ask Jesus what his vision for life was, he would have told you what he told the disciples, "The Son of Man must suffer many things and be rejected by the elders, chief priests and teachers of the law, and he must be killed and on the third day be raised to life."[2] Jesus's mission was to die. No fun and games there. The twelve disciples embraced the same mission and vision. Most of them were destined to die—no 401ks, no cushy success or prosperity for them. They followed Jesus to die.

Most of us will never have the opportunity to chart that path, but that should disappoint us, not relieve us. The book of Acts records a scene where the apostles were whipped and beaten for preaching the gospel. Luke reports their reaction: "The apostles left the Sanhedrin, rejoicing because they had been counted worthy of suffering disgrace for the Name."[3] These men and women rejoiced over the notion of suffering and possibly being martyred for Jesus Christ. Perhaps this is one reason the church was so powerful in the first century. John writes, "They overcame [Satan] by the blood of the Lamb and by the word of their testimony; they did not love their lives so much as to shrink from death."[4] Something about loving God more than life and being willing to suffer loss for the mission of Christ causes the defeat of Satan in life.[5]

Don't misunderstand me; we don't have to be this radical to bring delight to God. There's just something about you and me that makes him sing—irrespective of what we do.[6] This is great news, because the thing we tend to do best is botch things. God forgives us; we fall again. God gives us courage; we get discouraged. God gives us a dream; we make it a self-actualizing quest filled more with us than God. God gives us gifts; we go prodigal with them and use them for our own advantage. Let's face it; if we were God, we would kill us.

But God bases his decision to pursue us and work in us on *his* unconditional love. Unconditional love works without conditions—it isn't based on the actions of the one being loved. This God-love simply sets value and preciousness on us. It isn't an earned thing; it just *is*. We are loved because *we are*.

But running a bore-on, sold-out, race-to-the-cross kind of life is an option for any believer. And it's an option I want to pursue. I'm not talking about getting God to love me more or about securing a place in heaven—I'm talking about loving God with *all* my heart and mind and soul and strength because I think he is worth it. I'm talking about becoming a no-holds-barred disciple of Jesus Christ. I'm talking about embracing all those Bible verses that call us to deeper places not essential for salvation but essential for becoming prophetic to our culture—for bringing his voice into the earth. I'm talking about giving God more than he demands.

Pete Grieg asserts, "The greatest heroes of our faith have always been those like St. Francis of Assisi, Florence Nightingale, and Martin Luther King Jr., who responded to God's love with extraordinary personal sacrifice. But as I look around the Church at this time, I see a real danger looming: I am concerned that the message of grace, which is currently being propounded so passionately from pulpits and paperbacks around the world, might merely become a 'license to "chill"'— an all-embracing, one-size-fits-all, mindless rationale for accepting the greatest comfort and personal pleasure in any given situation. Such an aberration of grace labels those who break its code—those people who are seeking to be more disciplined and sacrificial in their faith—'religious,' 'pious,' 'driven,' 'culturally irrelevant,' 'caught up in good works,' 'perfectionistic,' or simply 'legalistic.'"[7]

Casual Christ-followers get to heaven—no doubt about it—but they don't get to change the world. Changing the world demands that people live differently.

Hot or Cold

"I know your deeds," Jesus tells a group of believers, "that you are neither cold nor hot. I wish you were either one or the other! So, because you are lukewarm—neither hot nor cold—I am about to spit you out of my mouth."[8]

As a kid, I heard this text preached over and over again. Red-faced preachers would yell, "You can't be lukewarm! God wants you to either be on fire for him or to hate him, but because you just sit there, you're going to get spit out—you're in danger of going to hell!"

That always made the crowd nervous and populated the altars. But something about it didn't sit right with me. Why would God rather have you "hate him" than to be a bit casual about him? And why would you merit hell for getting casual in your faith? Isn't going to heaven a free gift? Or is our message, "Accept Jesus, be red-hot for him, and you'll get into heaven—but if you relax and get lukewarm, you better wake up quick and get red-hot again or you're going to hell"?

I don't think Jesus is talking about going to hell or about being emotionally "on fire" for him versus hating him. I think he is talking about the idea that if you want to be a voice for him—to be his mouth in your world—you have to be willing to be different. Think about it. If you take a cup of boiling water and a glass of freezing-cold water and leave them in a room for several hours, what happens? The boiling water cools and the cold water warms. Eventually they both become the same temperature as that of the room. Neither sticks out. Both fit in. They become lukewarm.

I think Jesus is crying out to these believers, saying, "Don't try to fit in the world around you! Don't long to be the same. I want you to be hot about some things and cold about others. If you live like everyone else lives, you are the *same* as them. You can't stick out. You become the same temperature as those in the room with you—you are lukewarm. I won't be able to speak through you. I speak through those who are different. If you are unwilling to stand out, you won't be able to represent me—I will have to spit you out of my mouth."

No punishment of hell. No "God would rather have me hate him." He simply invites us to live transformed lives so we can speak for him. This is not essential for salvation, but it is essential for fulfilling destiny and mission—and that's the fun stuff.

Unnecessary Things

It takes lots of energy and work to become an active participant in the kingdom of God. Our willingness to embrace the kingdom does not produce salvation; it accepts a salvation relationship with God—a relationship that must be continually refreshed with the cultivation of the internal *yes* to God. We persistently "turn to God" so that "times of refreshing may come from the Lord."[9] And it impacts everything: how one relates to others, the world, and even one's self. But kingdom living is a scary, costly adventure. Why? Because it is a commitment to use grace, not only for ourselves but also for the others that God puts into our lives.[10]

Our first two boys are only about two years apart, and we always hauled them around together when they were little. There were many times at the mall when they both wanted the same things—like an ice cream cone—and we would get one for each of them. But there were other times when we didn't want them each to have one, but wanted them to *share*. Ah, sharing. Not a concept that is easily embraced by little boys (or by big ones, for that matter). But, to their horror, we asked them to do so anyway. We knew if they were to grow up as contributing adults and not third-world dictators they needed to learn how to share. Sharing develops a broader love of deeper things—a love of bringing joy to others.

Kingdom business is a bit like sharing your ice cream cone. When we say we want in on kingdom business, we are saying salvation is no longer about me getting my needs met; it's no longer about me being the only focus of God's attention. Kingdom business is about sharing with and focusing on others. Somehow focusing on others gives us a bridge to a transcendent life—access to a life that is bigger than one of our own crafting, a life that is bigger than the immediate desires of selfish people who seem only good at having ever-expanding needs. Sharing roots us in something grander, something bigger, something eternal. Taking on the needs and desires of others is a surrender to a reality beyond oneself—but it can be costly and painful! (Who naturally likes someone else licking his or her ice cream cone?)

In a world where nothing is considered more important than being number one, a life of focusing on others is seen as dangerous, maybe even crazy, because it is connected to something other than self. But focusing your life on others gives you a new self-worth based on an identity valued by God—it links our personal competency to fruitfulness for others.

But living for others is tough. This is why our desire and love for God tend to fade in our lives. This desire causes suffering, so after the pain kicks in we quite naturally shift the energy from a quest for eternal things and place it elsewhere, on "safer" things. Even when we set out to love God above all else, a gradual misplacement of energy usually occurs. Over time God seems rather elusive and distant, and earthly things are rather concrete and satisfying. Longing for what appears immediate, we repress the desire that demands more involvement with God and love of others. We avoid its price, although kingdom living is the most fulfilling. But there is a way to steady our involvement. Vow-making helps us stay the course for kingdom living.

Vow-making Is Practical

Making vows helps to steady the will's commitment to grace. Since the fall of the human race, the human will has been, at best, fickle. Fickle because the will is not connected to the eternal power and strength of grace but to the arbitrary whims or emotions of the human experience. We sit in church and hear a message preached or listen to a song or have a conversation with a respected mentor . . . and we feel convicted. We feel like we need to change and engage more with God and his purpose for the world. So, in the moment of *feeling*, we make a commitment. There are two problems with this. One, it is a commitment based on emotions, not eternal grace. And, two, this kind of commitment is focused on human performance instead of being focused on grace that releases divine energy for consistent right action.[11] Commitments based on emotions are always short lived. They die after the inspiration of the moment leaves. Such commitments are like the seashells strewn over an abandoned beach—seashells are places where life once was. Vow-making helps to connect the will to something other than the up and down of arbitrary human emotions.

Vows help us stick with the things we know are important. Let me revisit the fasting vow I mentioned in Chapter 6. Though this is a rather pale, trite example of following Jesus to die, it will help to show how vows help to curb our penchant to justify inaction. The faith community I am a part of decided to participate in corporate fasting on Wednesdays during the Lenten season this past year. There are a number of reasons why I do not like fasting. One, I like food. Two, I don't like the feeling I have when I don't eat food. Those are the big ones. But there are more. I don't like how grumpy I get when I don't get what I want . . . *food*. Fasting is a spiritual exposé for me—it exposes the little nasty attitudes that lurk deep in my soul, attitudes I can generally keep at bay in my more guarded moments. But not when I fast. Those lurking dragons crawl out into the light when I fast, and others see them. I can't cover them up.

Because I dislike fasting so much it is fairly easy for me to justify *not* fasting. There's the common: *I have to be ready for ministry, and since I do much ministry during lunch appointments, it would be a bad idea to commit to fasting during this 40-day period of Lent.* Or, *I need to get to the gym, and I can't go without any energy.* There was also the unmentionable, really selfish justification that Wednesdays are tortilla soup day at my favorite restaurant. There were many good reasons why I shouldn't fast with the community.

Because I knew how easy it would be to justify not participating, I entered a vow to fast with my community. (It was a private vow known only to God and me.) Why did I vow about this? Because vowing imitates the ancient warriors who burned their ships when they landed on the shores of lands they were to conquer. This act eliminated even the temptation to turn back from what they had determined to do. That's the *why* of vowing. Vowing simply helped steady my fidgety, self-justifying, hedonist-oriented will to stay the course.

Vows push us into the grace that helps us *do* what we believe is important for us to do. They are commitments to trust Christ to fill us with his grace and the power of the Holy Spirit. We are not supposed to vow in order to lock and load a jacked-up, naked commitment to *do* the thing we vowed to do. Doing is not even the point. The point is grace . . . we vow into grace. We vow to pursue the energy from God that enables consistency in our souls.

Remember the words of Paul, "But by the grace of God I am what I am, and his grace to me was not without effect. No, I worked harder than all of them—yet not I, but the grace of God that was with me."[12] Grace only succeeds when we pursue it—when we commit to saying *yes* to its presence in our lives. But even our efforts to embrace grace are born from a grace that produces that effort. Confusing? Kind of.

This might help. Grace is like the presence of a talent in your life, such as a talent for music. You may have musical talent in your soul, but untapped talent means nothing. It will not blossom or mature unless you are diligent. If you pursue your talent it will grow—it won't be "without effect." But working with it only succeeds because it is already there to work with. There is a "talent" of grace in the believer's soul, and we vow to tap into it.

When I woke on Wednesday mornings during this past Lenten season, I said to God, "Well, it's Wednesday—*tortilla soup Wednesday*. But I'm not going to eat today. I'm going to starve and deal with dragons. But I need your help. I'm asking you to help me reinterpret my hunger for food as a hunger for *you*! Thank you in advance for your grace that empowers me to do what is right. I'm going to be hungry for food today, but I am declaring that I am hungrier for you. I choose to love you more than food today. I vowed to this end, Lord. The ships are burned, and there's no way back, no way out. It's me and you. Let's do this together."

In this prayer encounter an exchange consistently happened, not unlike what Paul described when he wrote,

> [God] told me, "My grace is enough; it's all you need. My strength comes into its own in your weakness." Once I heard that, I was glad to let it happen. I quit focusing on the handicap and began appreciating the gift. It was a case of Christ's strength moving in on my weakness. Now . . . the weaker I get, the stronger I become.[13]

When you put money into a soda machine, your focus is not on the fact you are spending money; you have a view toward the end goal—the soda. You sacrifice your money anticipating the soda. Vows work the same way. Yes, there is a cost—a loss—and you've committed to an action of obedience. But the action is not what you are after. You're after the soda; you are anticipating grace. As you obey your vows, you anticipate that God will act; you just don't know where or when. But you listen and you continue to act in obedience as a gesture of your love and pursuit of God.

A vowed life is a life filled with a spirit of expectation that all good things will be given to the obedient heart—God will come.[14] And we are willing to lose our lives in the vow until we find it in Christ. This kind of life fills one with a spirit of self-worth grounded in values bigger than our solitary needs, wants, desires, and exaggerated sense of fairness and justice. Obedience that vow-making affords basically claims that we have a measure of responsibility for advancing God's cause in the world and that God will eventually arrive with his grace to help us follow through on that responsibility.

No Condemnation

Vow-making is *not* a commitment to perfection. I'm currently participating in a vow dealing with my health. I'm in my fifties and this old grey stallion (maybe gelding . . . yikes!) ain't what he used to be. I have sensed the conviction of the Holy Spirit nudging me to pay more attention to my health—what I eat and how much I exercise. My fickle will is all over the place on this one, so I have entered a vow in this regard. Honestly, this one has been tough. It's been kind of a hit-and-miss deal for me. There are so many issues involved from my ever-changing schedule to the weather to the soul-comfort of food to the dread I feel about the thought of exercise. There are more than a few species of dragons previously unknown to me that have shown up in my soul in this vowing enterprise. Complex indeed.

Up until recently I was not doing well—too many hamburgers, lots of barbeque, and too many hours of sedentary activity with only my fingers doing the walking on my computer keyboard. But true vows are never immobilized by guilt for past disobedience, nor are they caught up in excessive self-righteousness when the vow is kept. The focus is not on the "self" at all but on the promotion of the kingdom of God. True, when obedience fails there is a sense of regret or remorse. I hated that I had lost ground in the health vow I had made, but I was not deterred. Instead of letting my feelings of regret and remorse for failed obedience drive me into an unhealthy guilt and condemnation, I reinterpreted them as a call to stay accountable to the vow I had made. In the face of failure vow-making fosters a healthy spirit of repentance that is not self-depreciating but life-confirming.

Always remember that the real goal of vow-making is not perfection; it is an ongoing motion toward God in a spirit of humility. Vow-making gives us the freedom to take initiative, make mistakes, and still stay bonded in union with the vowed promise. Living like this gives us a deep sense of personal purpose and vocation. We become cheerful participants in the scheme of creation and of God's providence that grounds us in a sense of purpose and dedication.

Just the other day I met with a couple who wanted to renew their wedding vows. They had had a rough year of transition and conflict and they wanted to reaffirm their vows to love and cherish and place each other's needs above their own. They knew they wouldn't be perfect at it. That wasn't the point. They knew they would have days when they would wake up selfish and violate the law of love, but they still wanted to renew their precious marital vow. Why? Because they got what vowing means—that it isn't so much a promise to perfection as it is a promise to continue moving toward each other in a spirit of humility and commitment no matter what. They knew they were vowing into relationship, not performance. They knew on days when their obedience to their vows failed, they would feel a sense of regret or remorse—but they were looking forward to those feelings as forms of "accountability." They understood vows are a ship-burning exercise. They understood that their vows were a promise to continue moving toward each other even if they make mistakes. They knew their vowed promise would allow them to stay bonded through their imperfections because it is a promise to live beyond self.

Mini-muggings and Living Vines

Why do we vow? Because most often our human emotions can only get us to the land of good intentions. We intend to do what we believe we should do, but we just don't do it. Vows demand a "yes," irrespective of feelings. Vows are mini-muggings. They say to the will, "I don't care what you want to do today, we are going to the cross of Christ." Vowing is deciding in advance; it's refusing to let your decisions be managed by your emotions. True, there is a resistance to this kind of thing in our culture—to any kind of pre-decision-making. We want things to stay open-ended to the very last moment; then we can do what we truly "feel" like doing at all times. People value a kind of personal "drifting" and see it as a form of freedom, but the truth is that this kind of radical open-endedness results in a sense of aimlessness and inferiority. Alienation and anxiety result from our inability to choose and submit our energies to the choices we make.

There is a quest in the human soul for a significant future. Vows help us get there. Vows are "futuring" projects. They have eschatological significance—they have a view of God's rule being present here and now, not just there and then. They help us participate in "the powers of the coming age."[15] We vow into those powers as a gesture of our faith in the prayer, "Thy kingdom come. Thy will be done in earth, as it is in heaven."[16]

In vowing we are embracing a new rule for our lives. The Monastic tradition developed a concept called the "Rule of Life." The Rule, whatever form it took, was always intended to help guide the faithful in a way of living that was deeply congruent with God and his will for human life. The word "rule" comes from the Latin *regula*. The origins of *regula* had to do with a trellis in a garden. A trellis is a structure on which vines and other garden plants can wrap themselves and climb off of the ground by attaching themselves to it.

The trick to vowing is to find the "trellises" that make sense for you in terms of who you are and where you're at in your walk of faith. Then you order your life around those trellises, knowing that as you do so, you're providing a structure within which your spirituality can flourish. But the vowing isn't made with a view only to structure but to the relationship that can be deepened because of the structure. Remember, the goal is not the accomplishment of the thing vowed but the experience of the relationship that develops as you participate in the vow.

One can argue that we already have a relationship with Christ without vowing. And I would agree. But the relationship we have with Christ is often more a relationship of potential than one of deep communion—communion requires growth. Think of the myriad potentialities for growth that can happen when the human person is interfaced with the Person of God! We all know there is *more*; vows help us uncover the *more*.

And those who say structure is bondage are being silly at best, selfish and self-delusional at worst. Despite all of our clever arguments to the contrary ("I have relationship and not religion!"), all relationships require structure. Without structure we become terminal neophytes—we never really get the point of kingdom mission. Or even worse, we become Jabba-the-Huts in the church—consuming, consuming, consuming (and growing, no doubt about that). But we are not growing in any way that is productive or transformational, just growing into a blob of fatness without the bones and musculature to make good use of what is consumed.

A person gripped by the reality of God in Christ will know intuitively that they must participate in some kind of order or rule of life in order to see that reality deepen—they must crack open the Scriptures, pray, fellowship with other believers, move toward leading a morally sound life, and so on. These are trellises without which the vines of our budding spirituality would merely creep along the ground not bearing much fruit. The *regula* helps take this intuition seriously in terms of our own personal uniqueness and calling, with the result that a "rule of life" (composed of a variety of vows) is person-specific, extending beyond "the basics" to a whole host of intentional rhythms which guide an individual's spiritual growth in the way that God intends! This is the fodder of a robust spiritual life.

So, how does vowing actually work? What do we vow about? When is it appropriate to make vows and when is it not appropriate to do so? And how do we vow? What do we say? Who should be there? Who should know? These are all great questions that need to be considered. Let's begin by looking at the anatomy of vow-making next.

10. The Anatomy of Vow-making

I am bound by the vow I made to you, O God.
—Ps. 56:12

In our age, when we think of vows we generally think of the ones made in marriage or the vows made by the religious (priests, monks, and nuns). We know that those who participate in such vows are destined for a new kind of living—their lives are altered by the vows they make. And we are rightfully suspicious that all vows bring a change in how one lives— which implies they need to be approached with thoughtfulness and caution (presumably any kind of "Las Vegas" vowing would be dangerous).

When I first began to unearth this whole vow-making enterprise, I couldn't help but wonder why both the Old and New Testaments mention vows without much in the way of specific instruction regarding them. In his book *Celebration of Discipline*, Richard Foster makes the point that, though the Bible addresses ancient practices like solitude and fasting, it gives "almost no instruction about how to do them." He explains that the Bible doesn't give specific instructions because these "were so frequently practiced and such a part of the general culture that the 'how to' was common knowledge."

It turns out that the same holds true for vow-making. During the time when the New Testament was written, its writers saw no need to explain the "why" or "how" of vow-making. But the fact that Scripture does not give us specifics about vowing does not mean it is an invalid practice any more than the absence of specific instructions in the New Testament about how to participate in solitude invalidates that practice. The truth is, these things were so common in the everyday experience of the people that they needed no specific instruction on how or why they should fast or vow—they just did it.

As we pointed out in Chapter 1, the practice of vow-making was commonplace in the early church. Making vows was about as popular as prayer and worship gatherings. Scholars claim the making of vows was practiced by ordinary people all through biblical history, as well as in most religions in the societies surrounding them.[1]

Vows are things a Christian may, out of his or her own free impulse, promise to God. They may be certain special acts a person decides to participate in, or ways in which he or she chooses to live for a limited period of time or for a lifetime. Vows emerge from the domain of free will and are the result of an impulse of one's devotion to God. Please keep in mind that if you never participate in a "vow" you still get to go to heaven and God will love you no less. However, I am convinced that the ancient practice of vowing can really help tether our twenty-first-century, helter-skelter lives to the eternal.

But how does one go about making a vow?

Vow-making

Let's look at twelve things you should keep in mind as you approach the vowing practice.

1. A vow is an act of generosity toward God. As we have pointed out, vows are not a mandated aspect of our worship of God—they are extras, commitments beyond what is necessary or required. This is because vows, by definition, are in the domain of personal choice. God does not expect them and, hence, they are not codified in Scripture. Perhaps this is precisely the reason vow-making is so transformational. The unnecessary things we do in any relationship, from friendships to marriage to our faith life, seem to add strength and freshness to that relationship.

Over the past thirty-plus years in my relationship with Gail, it has been the unnecessary, unexpected flowers, calls, gifts, and surprises that I have given her that have seemed to enrich our marriage the most—unexpected things bring fresh wind into a loving relationship. To be sure, these gestures are a kind of secret-in-the-sauce for a lifelong romance. I think vowed acts do the same thing in the arena of faith as well.

But be careful. The point of vowing is love for God, not altering your behavior (though your behavior *is* altered through vowing). If you enter the arena of vowing for the wrong reason (to make God happier with you, to be more holy, to be a better Christian, to make God more inclined to give you something, and so on), you will make your life of faith harder instead of sweeter. Vowing has nothing to do with trying to get God to love you more or about trying to become a "better" Christian. Participating in vows of dedication will not make you a special saint; there is no room for elitism in the kingdom. Actually, vowing isn't about us trying to get anything at all—it's about loving God beyond what he asks. It is about identifying and promising to participate in activities that move us more and more deeply into the rhythm of the kingdom of God. Not because we have to, but because we want to. It's about doing things that cultivate a consistent, resounding *yes* in our hearts before God.

Don't let a misguided quest to get God to love you more be at the core of why you are trying to vow. Always remember God loves you no matter what. You are accepted no matter what. The cross guarantees that you and I are at all times claimed by God's love. God's forgiving love is the reason any one of us gets to belong; it's not the consequence of human performance. A vow can quickly become bondage as easily as it can release joy into a deeper relationship with God—perhaps even more easily.

Whenever we make altering behavior our end in vowing, the activity is quickly reduced to nothing more than a kind of clinical anal retentiveness masquerading as religious piety—not a thing of faith at all. This has nothing to do with loving God more. This is legalism trying to encroach once again on Christian freedom. True vow-making is simply our choosing to add permanence to what we have learned to do out of a love for God. The reason I decided to vow about doing the Daily Office, where I take four to five God-breaks a day with prayer and Scripture reading (see Chapter 4), is because I *loved* doing it and because I felt the smile of heaven in my soul as I did. It wasn't hard to do. I didn't "vow" to continue doing it because I was trying to impress God, nor was I trying to force myself to keep doing something I hated but thought God wanted.

If you cannot consistently do what it is you want to vow to do out of a simple love for God, you have no business trying to vow into the behavior in the first place. You should only vow to things commensurate with the way you want to love God—with things that are in accord with where your soul is and with what you can easily bear. If you are not careful to follow these guidelines, vow-making will hurt your faith more than help it.

2. Vowing presupposes the full consent of the will. The most well-known vow is the vow of marriage. And much of what we can say about vows in general, we can extrapolate from the marital vow. For example, marriage should never be entered into forcefully. The marital vow is only valid when there is the joyful consent of both parties involved—a marriage vow should be the fruit of a generous will eager to give and a willingness to sacrifice beyond what is necessary.

A shotgun wedding does not lend itself to "generosity"—it is a type of wedding that is arranged, not because of the desire of the participants, but by coercion. "Shotgun wedding" is the expression used to refer to a hasty marriage arranged due to some happening or event (such as unplanned pregnancy) which forces a couple to marry when they would have chosen otherwise under different circumstances. Their vows are generally not considered legitimate in this context because one cannot be forced into vowing.

There can be no external pressure pushing you to enter a vow beyond what you would have chosen to do without that pressure. And just like a marriage can be jeopardized when a couple marries for the wrong reasons, a vow in the context of faith can be jeopardized if you are vowing for the wrong reasons. There are scads of wrong reasons for participating in the vow of marriage: Some marry in the hope that getting married will make them happy or make them feel "whole," but the truth is happy and emotionally whole singles make happy and emotionally whole "marrieds," while miserable and emotionally needy singles make marriage a miserable, lonely proposition. Others enter the marriage vow because they want to make their partner happy or they feel like they "owe it" to the other person. Some marry in order to meet the expectations of friends, relatives, or because they want to "fit in" with the married crowd. Still others marry because they feel marriage guarantees that they will be loved, and they really, really want to be loved. But these are all bad reasons to enter a vow of marriage. All vows are about free will; they have nothing to do with external intimidation or undue influence.

If you vow in the arena of faith because you feel forced into it (because you want to "fit in" or because you think you "owe it" to God), rather than because you choose to do so from the heart, it will reduce you to slavery. Vowing is to be born out of an enthusiasm afforded by a generous will, never the result of pressure. Pressure will only lead to the grudging service of involuntary enslavement. Not good.

Entering into a vow under duress will only make faith more difficult. This is why wisdom demands (and the Bible warns) that you enter into any vow wisely, thoughtfully, and with an appropriate degree of fear—fully realizing that you do not have to participate in a vow if you are not so inclined. Many are too young in the faith to participate in vow-making, simply because they don't really understand what it is they are attempting to do. If that's the case, any vow they enter into is not really valid—it is null and void by virtue of ignorance. The one who can say sincerely, "If I had known this or that, I would not have made the vow," is not bound by a vow.

3. We vow to God. As couples enter the marital vow, they hold the other person as the focus or point of the vow. When we vow to God, he needs to be the focus. We vow to *know* him, not just to *do* for him. Spouses make vows to each other in order to make permanent their choice to develop and grow in love with each other. Vows in faith do the same thing. We vow because we are choosing to continue doing the things we have discovered help us develop and grow in love with God. Vows make the actions of love—the duties we believe are important—permanent and irrevocable. Just as the marriage vow provides a framework for giving the actions of love between a couple a future, vows in our faith provide a framework to give our loving actions toward God a future—we seek to hold in the present a framework for our relationship with God, and it is one defined concretely enough that it will endure in the future.

Though vows do not add to nor contradict our salvation experience, they do specify it. Vow-making gives new direction to our lives by giving God a new claim over us. As is true with newlyweds, we may only have a glimmer of what the vow really means when we first make it, but it begins to shape us over time. Margaret Farley puts it this way: "Commitment is love's way of being whole while it still grows into wholeness."[2]

Though God is due the dedication of *all* our actions by our surrender to Jesus as Lord, by adding "vows" to our surrender we declare that God deserves more than he demands. This is why vows are more than an attempt to get us to live right, moderately, and normally—that alone misses the point of vow-making. Vows are about deepening our pursuit of the Holy One—this is where our souls follow hard after God,[3] and where we decide to "weary ourselves" in our pursuit of God,[4] beyond what is required or expected.

4. Vows are a weighty enterprise. Count the cost. The instant we use the word "vow" there should be a little note of dread in us. Vows are weighty, if not downright scary. Solomon wrote, "It is better not to vow than to make a vow and not fulfill it."[5] Vows are promises made directly to God (we're not talking about New Year's resolutions here). Vows are promises you make from which there is no retreat—remember, they imitate the ancient warriors who burned their ships to cut off the possibility to run from battle. You are committed when you enter a vow to God. This is why they must not be entered into lightly.

But most Americans are in trouble in the "keeping your word" department. We are a flip-flop culture—you can have a strong opinion about something one day and completely change your mind the next. And that is considered completely OK; nobody bats an eye. We are part of an ideologically disposable and ever-changing society. It is "odd" for people to stand firm in their convictions—that crowd is seen as "close-minded." As a result, the average American feels he or she can make commitments and then back out of them whenever they become too hard to keep.

Even the marital vow has become a pretty pale enterprise. Think of the young couples entering marriage today. When a vowing young couple says, "I promise to love and cherish you," to each other, they are really thinking something more like "I promise *I will try*." For many, the marriage vow comes with a prenuptial "out" implied. Our society really doesn't see a vow as something that is irrevocable. We have lost our capacity for integrity.

For the first hundred and fifty years of American history, American writers claimed that the key to success in any venture (including marriage) was in the development of our interior life—our character. Traits like honesty, integrity, perseverance, kindness, courage, moderation, patience, industry, and so on, were seen as essential ingredients for a happy life. But about eighty years ago a change in emphasis began to emerge. Instead of hinging success on internal character building, writers, lecturers, and educators began to focus on externals like good communication, courteous mannerisms (such as smiling, eye contact, firm handshakes), positive attitudes, developing good listening skills—all things that helped you make friends and influence people.

These things are not bad in and of themselves, and are, in fact, helpful in cultivating success, but their development needs to be built on one's character, not to be a replacement for it or a cover up for bad character. When one uses external techniques to disarm and influence people when they are of ignoble character, it becomes flat-out manipulation—this guy or gal smiles, listens, and extends kindness to people simply to gain an advantage over them. Characterless schmoozing always causes people to feel used.

Vow-making transcends this trend. We do not have to make vows, but when we do Scripture says, "This is what God commands: When a man makes a vow to God . . . he must not break his word; he must do exactly what he has said."[6] We don't vow and then give up when it is no longer easy to keep the vow. Nor can we justify that we really were *trying*, which should be enough. Trying isn't enough for the vow maker; only *doing* counts.

5. Vows do not apply to things directly commanded by God. We are not to vow about things directly commanded in Scripture. For example, no one should make a vow to avoid sin because God already commands us to avoid sin. However, we may vow to participate in things that support our obedience to direct commands. For example, if you recognize you have a tendency to make food too central in your life—that the sin of gluttony finds a home in you more often than you'd like—you may want to vow to do things that help you steer further away from the gravitational pull of that sin (like vowing not to watch the food channel or not to stash desserts all over the kitchen). Vows like these can aid your weak will as you search for, discover, and begin to practice the grace God has for you to control your food impulse.

Likewise, a dating couple might get to the point where they keep slipping closer and closer to inappropriate physical contact and they don't want to fall into sin. They cannot vow not to sin, but they can vow to keep themselves out of situations where sinning is easier (that is, vow to only be "alone" in public, or to stay vertical and not lay around the house playing kissy-face too much, and so on).

Scripture claims we are free from the dominion of sin.[7] You and I do not have to live under the control of things like greed and envy and lust and anger and addiction—Jesus died to break the power of the things that tend to nail us and get us stuck. But the "way out" that God affords us[8]—the grace pathways—

must be sought, understood, and diligently practiced. This is where vow-making can help.

You cannot vow that you will not sin, but you can vow to do whatever you must (study, pray, counsel, and so on) for however long it takes to discover the escape plan God claims is there for you. God is the one who has promised he will not allow you to be "tempted beyond what you can bear" and that he will "provide a way out so that you can stand up under" the temptation to sin.[9] Vowing guarantees you will keep searching and running at this promise until you figure out how to get it functioning in your life. Vowing is your promise to "not to receive God's grace in vain."[10] It is your commitment to "be strong in the grace that is in Christ Jesus."[11]

6. Vows can be added to "duties" already being practiced. There are a host of practices we do—from regular prayer to consistently walking in the love of God toward others to being involved in some kind of ministry endeavor—that can be vowed into. We are commanded to pray, but we are not told how much. We are told to walk in love, but there are so many ways to skirt around that—such as avoiding some person we'd rather not deal with at the moment. We are invited into mission and ministry, but how much we get involved or which area of ministry we participate in are not mandated. There is much room for "personal choice" even in mandated areas of our faith—and whenever personal choice presents itself, vow-making becomes an option. The object of a vow, according to the classical formula, is not merely doing something good but doing what you are already doing under the impulse of grace, only better.

The reason vowing is helpful is because we all have fickle,

emotion-ruled wills that fight against being consistent over just about anything—particularly anything mandated. (Remember, the will loves to be self-moving!) With this kind of will always struggling for dominion in our souls, kingdom participation does not come with ease. Consequently sincere Christians often love God like they get the measles—in *spots*. When a sermon or a worship service inspires them to action, they glow bright. But it isn't long before the "glory" wears off and their love wanes and the action stops—they love in spots.

Vowing helps push past this. We vow because we want to make some specific duty permanent (at least for the duration of the vow). Vowing helps because it effectively usurps the propensity of our fickle will from resigning duties we believe we should practice after we experience the loss of the inspired feelings we had about those duties or when the duty becomes significantly difficult. Vows steady the will; they are pre-decisions based on principles and values, not the erratic up-and-down feelings that plague most of us. We vow to things in order to stay tethered to our commitments when we no longer want to keep them. They help us stick even when it hurts.

We need to practice what God commands because it prepares us for participating in the *missio Dei*—the mission of God in the earth. Vowing into consistency in any mandated practice can prove to be a "mission saver." Paul wrote, "It is required that those who have been given a trust must prove faithful."[12] Representing God and his kingdom doesn't *just happen*. The Bible gives us images of becoming a good soldier of Christ Jesus,[13] a disciplined athlete,[14] a hardworking farmer,[15] and so on, as it describes those who pull back from what other, normal, everyday people do in order to participate in the Master's work.

Making choices to say no to some things in order to say yes to the things God calls us to is what vow-making is all about. Vows help us hone in on consistency and faithfulness—critical issues for participation in God's kingdom. Jesus said, "No one who puts his hand to the plow and looks back is fit for service in the kingdom of God."[16]

The invitation is always laid out there for us to become more serious in the way we follow God. Remember, Jesus had followers at various levels: there were the "crowds" that followed him,[17] the "seventy-two others" Jesus sent "two by two ahead of him to every town and place where he was about to go,"[18] the twelve apostles, and his inner circle of Peter, James, and John.[19] I think we determine how close to Jesus we want to be—the "level" we want to live at. How deeply we want to live in the kingdom of God isn't forced upon us.

A person who wants to change the world must work hard at cultivating a consistent *praxis,* or practice of faith, in order to become a "vessel" God can use to advance his kingdom. Paul wrote, "In a wealthy home some utensils are made of gold and silver, and some are made of wood and clay. The expensive utensils are used for special occasions, and the cheap ones are for everyday use. If you keep yourself pure, you will be a special utensil for honorable use. Your life will be clean, and you will be ready for the Master to use you for every good work."[20] Do you want to be an "expensive utensil" used by God for "special occasions" or do you want to be some "cheap" paperware? In this regard, you choose how you want to be utilized, not God.

Sadly, our culture is not really open to anything as horrifyingly *un*pleasurable as discipline and commitment. We are way too self-indulgent. We believe the world is here for our own

129

liberty, and we feel we should be allowed to "get away with" doing whatever it is we want, whenever we want to. And ours is an instantaneous culture. We have come to expect things instantly. We like fast diets, overnight success, rapid fitness, a hundred-yard dash to marital bliss, and one altar call to power. If we don't experience what we want in a reasonable amount of time—say a day or two—we think something is wrong.

Those of us over fifty were once called the "now generation"—we were pretty well known for how easy it was for us to quit before the rewards showed up—jobs, educational paths, relationships, pretty much anything complex or difficult. Why? We couldn't have it *now*. Sadly, the generations that follow us expect no less. Since the '60s millions of children have been raised with no idea of how to sacrifice for other people. Our society has glorified the do-what-feels-right-for-you mantra to such an extreme that most don't even *understand* the concept of selflessness, much less *practice* it. Most enter jobs, marriages, friendships, decisions, whatever, with a "what's in it for me?" mentality. All they are interested in is "Gimme this. Gimme that. Gimme what I want." We have developed a whole generation of "gimme" monsters. The "Me, Me, Me Gimme monster" lifestyle is ultimately destructive and anti-kingdom. People like this can hardly get along with themselves, much less with other human beings.

Life for the Christian is supposed to be built on a completely different footing than feelings or the "what do I get out of this?" mindset. It's to be built on the likes of sacrifice, discipline, obedience, persistence, and so on. But most in our culture are not oriented to governing their lives by things like courage or commitment. Americans are prone to being controlled by feelings (as evidenced by our hedonistic lifestlye) and are generally committed only to convenience and ease. For most, when the going gets tough they just quit. That's why I believe leaders and those involved in discipleship-making should consider implementing vow-making in their efforts. I'm convinced it can be extremely helpful in a cultural milieu like ours.

Let's continue unpacking the anatomy of vow-making by considering the role the Holy Spirit plays in this context.

11. The Anatomy of Vow-making, Part Two

I am bound by the vow I made to you, O God;
I will present to you thank-offerings.
Ps. 56:11[1]

In our last chapter, we began looking at the twelve things you should keep in mind as you approach the vowing practice. Let's continue.

7. When making vows, be led by the Holy Spirit. A number of years ago I decided to take the time to listen to a few Christian telev sion and radio programs to catch what the preachers were telling us to do. The first program I tuned into was a Christian talk show where a woman was telling the host: "I never let my husband see me without my being dressed in something cute, my hair made up, and my makeup on. I think Christian women need to go out of their way to make sure they are presentable to the head of their home! We are to treat our husbands as Christ, you know. And what woman wouldn't want to look her best for Jesus?" And she used some pretty good Bible verses to nail down her claims (which effectively "nailed" the women listening). It was probably just a coincidence that she was a newlywed with no children and that most of the women watching that mid-morning were probably at-home moms with little children clawing at their legs by the crack of dawn. I imagined if her listeners took her word as gospel, most of them would have to get up by 4:00 AM to pull off looking like a beauty queen before their "mom" duties kicked in.

On the very next program another woman was ranting about how important it is for Christian women to keep their houses clean. She talked about how meticulous she was about vacuuming, keeping clutter out of the closets, cleaning the bathrooms, and claimed she even did the "white glove" test over the refrigerator—all while explaining that she felt dirty homes were a sign of "spiritual dirtiness" and the reason why some marriages fall apart. (I'm sure you can just imagine the encouragement being channeled through the TV signal during *that* interview.) It was probably just a coincidence that this lady was an "empty-nester" who was married to a guy who sounded like a persnickety neat freak who never left anything laying around. Who cares that the majority of the women listeners probably lived with a gaggle of "messies" and that it was likely those gals couldn't find a white glove around their cluttered worlds if their lives depended on it.

Then I listened to a Christian psychologist who claimed Christian parents should have a deep, personal, intimate relationship with each of their children. And he proceeded to talk about how he enjoyed that with his children. It was probably just a coincidence that he only had two and that many of the parents listening had four or more.

Back-to-back with the Christian psychologist came another very popular preacher who began his message by citing the verse where Jesus asked his disciples, "Could you not pray with me for one hour?"[2] He then proceeded to assert that one wasn't a true follower of Christ unless he prayed for at least one hour a day.

It was then that I thought about the poor woman who was catching all these shows . . . trying to dutifully obey God by getting up hours before her husband in order to beautify herself; desperately following her debris-scattering family members in order to obviate "spiritual dirtiness"; all while attempting to schedule deep, personal, intimate encounters with her seven children in between driving to soccer matches and dance classes, cleaning above the refrigerator, buying groceries and cooking dinner (not to mention her need to adjust her life in response to the "call" she's getting from her local church to be "more involved" in the work of the Lord); *plus* she needs to make sure she has at least one hour of special prayer time to keep Christ happy. Hmm. Obvious fodder for total burnout, if not going completely insane. And that is precisely where many believers are—they are emotional and spiritual crispy-critters.

I'm not saying the Christian voices in the media have nothing good to say; they do. I'm saying if you *just* listen to them (or your pastor, for that matter) to get your marching orders for faith, you will go crazy. Christians aren't supposed to get their orders from the preachers—we are supposed to learn to hear the voice of the Holy Spirit. This is what the apostle John was referring to when he wrote, "You do not need anyone to teach you. But as his anointing teaches you about all things and as that anointing is real . . ."[3] The "anointing" is the presence of the Holy Spirit upon your life and mind. Though God uses teachers and preachers, they are not to usurp the role of the Holy

Spirit in your life. In fact, you are to listen for the Holy Spirit as those teachers and preachers talk.

In the arena of faith, getting to know the Holy Spirit is not an option—not if you want to prevent burnout and insanity. When Jesus was getting ready to physically leave this planet, he made a striking statement about the Holy Spirit. He said, "But I tell you the truth: It is for your good that I am going away. Unless I go away, the Counselor will not come to you; but if I go, I will send him to you."[4] Jesus was saying that his disciples would be better off if he was not physically on this planet! That had to be sort of hard to believe. As long as Jesus was around, he taught them how to pray.[5] He explained the Bible to them.[6] He gave them direction for their lives.[7] He showed them the power of God.[8] How could it be to their advantage for him to leave?

The answer is in his promise to send "the Comforter," the Holy Spirit. Now he, the Holy Spirit, teaches us how to pray: "But you, dear friends, build yourselves up in your most holy faith and pray in the Holy Spirit."[9] Now the Holy Spirit explains the Bible to us: "But when he, the Spirit of truth, comes, he will guide you into all truth."[10] Now the Holy Spirit gives us direction for our lives: "Those who are led by the Spirit of God are sons of God."[11] Now the Holy Spirit brings us the power of God: "But you will receive power when the Holy Spirit comes on you."[12]

Jesus showed the disciples that what he had been to them while he was physically present, the Holy Spirit would be, and more! To connect with Jesus in those days you had to wait in line—you also had to find where the line was—he was pretty elusive.[13] But Jesus promised that the Holy Spirit would be as close as a prayer to an open heart. No hunting him down. No long lines to wait in. The Holy Spirit is God being always-and-everywhere-present to the believer.

Before you run gung-ho in the direction of vow-making, pray and ask the Holy Spirit to guide you. God knows us better than we know ourselves. Pray about the area you are considering vowing in. Ask God to give you a soul-audit to see if this is the right time for you to enter a vow. He knows when to put the pressure on and when you should avoid all forms of additional pressure. Believe it or not people can get too "religious" and move into spiritual commitments for the wrong reasons—they push themselves in a way that makes their efforts more of a vice than a virtue. They embrace a kind of spiritual gluttony and nearly kill themselves with over-devotion to spiritual exercises. It's often better for these people to give up their devotions entirely, at least for a season. Jesus promised to send us the Holy Spirit to help each of us on a unique path that speaks to our lives, our gifts and callings, and our unique journeys in life.

Ask the Holy Spirit to help you be discerning as you engage in the vowing enterprise. Ask him to help you be honest about whether or not you have experienced enough grace in this area to vow into it (see Chapter 3). Are you are ready for a vow? Ask him if the timing is right. Ask him to help you keep your motives right. As we have been saying, never enter a vow to be a better Christian or because others at church are doing it or to overcome some wrong behavior in your life or to get God to love you more, and so on. The psalmist wrote, "Search me, O God, and know my heart; test me and know my anxious thoughts. See if there is any offensive way in me, and lead me in the way everlasting."[14] Pray this prayer. The Holy Spirit *will* lead you.

If all you get is confusion as you pray about this, don't move forward. God is *not* the author of confusion,[15] and confusion might be a sign that something isn't right—the timing, your understanding, *something*. Vowing is a serious thing. Make sure the Holy Spirit is smack in the middle of the vows you enter. True, you are the one *choosing* to vow, but God is really smart—much smarter than you—and he sees what's ahead. Let him lead you. Vows are not just things we do; they are an openness to the God who saves, who engages the human heart, and who draws near to us when we draw near to him.[16]

Remember that vow-making is a gesture or channel for you to love God back—it's a form of worship. Vows are born from an intentional desire within the believer to allow God's Spirit to penetrate the various facets of his or her life in real time and space. They are promises that hope to shape our futures for the glory of God. To leave out the central role of the Holy Spirit in vow-making is to make vows mechanical acts done in disregard to the spirit of worship.

8. Vows are sacrificial in nature. The Scripture says, "[Jesus] learned obedience from what he suffered."[17] Though suffering is not something we moderns ever think to embrace, it does have its upside. The writer of Hebrews talked about the suffering associated with maturing in our faith: "No discipline seems pleasant at the time, but painful. Later on, however, it produces a harvest of righteousness and peace for those who have been trained by it."[18] Peter claimed if you are willing to suffer while doing good "the Spirit of glory and of God rests on you."[19]

In a very real way, vows willingly embrace suffering—you are vowing to do things that don't come *easy* (like a special season of prayer, time of fasting, period of silence, season of chastity, time of study, and so on). Each vow involves a commitment to do something and a promise to refrain from doing something else. In this sense vowing is a kind of self-abandonment—we are committing to live beyond the desires of self. Vows are gestures to de-center from the "self" in order to trust God to take over the center of the self—to give control over one's life to the domain of God. This is why living within the framework of vowing is to step into the freedom of loving God with your whole heart.

But this requires pushing off and ignoring what the Bible refers to as "the flesh,"[20] which presents a problem. The flesh refers to our *cravings*. To suggest we should curb, much less deny, our cravings in some kind of vowed practice is met with gasps of unbelief, if not outright outrage in a modern, hedonistic society. Resisting cravings and longings appears prima facie wrong to the modern mind. Why would we want to push against what we consider the gateway to happiness: the sacred senses?

But Jesus said, "God is spirit, and his worshipers must worship in spirit and in truth."[21] Jesus is telling us that God is beyond the flesh, beyond what we can see. And he is telling us that if we want to be his worshipers, we have to approach God differently than we approach one another—we must approach him "in spirit." Whatever we take "in spirit" to mean, it does imply something beyond the dimension of the body and its impulses and demands. This would pose a challenge to any of us because it would mean moving down a path that ignores or even denies the mandates of the body. And, at least in my experience, the body never submits without a fight!

Paul speaks to this, "For the flesh lusts against the Spirit, and the Spirit against the flesh; and these are contrary to one another, so that you do not do the things that you wish."[22] Paul concludes that this fight can only be settled by the body being mercilessly crucified: "And they that are Christ's have crucified the flesh with the affections and lusts."[23] This "crucifixion" of flesh appears to be a kind of asceticism—asceticism is the notion that a person can attain a high spiritual and moral state by practicing self-denial, self-mortification, and the like. Ooooh, can't you just feel your flesh crawling at the thought of that idea. But this asceticism is a crucifixion that purifies the heart by conquering the supremacy of the body, allowing the spirit to commune with God.

From a subjective, experiential standpoint, it appears that we have a spiritual component that has a different set of demands than the demands of the body. Further, it seems that many of the bodily desires are harmful to our spiritual lives and must be kept under control. Vowing into sacrifice is to refuse to allow bodily appetites to control or dominate the human life. This does something to prepare one's heart that rumors John the Baptist's call to "Prepare the way for the Lord, make straight paths for him."[24] This is the point of vow-making.

Vows are commitments to emptying ourselves in order to be filled with God. The virgin womb of Mary was not empty as an end but empty to be ready to receive life and to bring that life into the world. In vowing, we empty ourselves of our control and the right to choose our own path in order to secure God's control and to find divine wholeness, authenticity, and freedom in the love of God. But giving up control has pain and suffering written all over it. Sadly, the concept of *intentional* sacrifice within the context of vowed living is a hard sell for the Western church.

In smorgasbord fashion, many in the church tend to only focus on promises like, "I can do all things through Christ,"[25] or "In all these things we are more than conquerors through him who loved us,"[26] or "I wish above all things that thou mayest prosper and be in health, even as thy soul prospereth."[27] But this same group often ignores verses like, "And anyone who does not take his cross and follow me is not worthy of me,"[28] or "Therefore, since Christ suffered in his body, arm yourselves also with the same attitude, because he who has suffered in his body is done with sin,"[29] or "And the God of all grace, who called you to his eternal glory in Christ, after you have suffered a little while, will himself restore you and make you strong, firm and steadfast."[30]

When people trained by a self-indulgent culture cross the threshold of faith and begin to follow Christ, they tend to only see proof-texts that promise joy and abundance, while completely missing those that call them to sacrifice and suffering. Why? They just don't see them. "Victory," "abundance," "power," "more," and "bigger" are words that best capture the expectations they have—to demand anything "less" is seen as compromise. And they don't compromise, at least not on this point. Ergo, self-indulgence continues to rule.

But vow-making fronts self-indulgence and pushes us into the risky world of selflessness, which imitates Christ's journey to the cross (the "paschal journey"). In a real way vows cause us to participate in the paschal gesture of surrender and obedience. As we use our freedom to follow a pathway of love, our freedom is gradually and steadily "lost." Our choices push freedoms out, but instead of feeling loss and restriction within our hearts, we experience new levels of freedom within. It turns out that he who loses his life, finds it.[31] This, however, is not the destruction of autonomy. It is the preservation and transformation of it by taking it up into the dominion of the kingdom of God. Here we meet God, learn to love, and experience true fulfillment. This is more than moving from bad habits to good habits. It is moving the rhythm of our lives into Christ, where we become new creations in him.[32]

Though sacrifice is intrinsic to vow-making, make sure you pray about the sacrifice involved before you enter a vow. A vow is like a coin. On one side there is a kind of giving up, on the other side is the entering into a deeper love relationship with God and others. If you are more aware of what you are giving up than you are of the deepening love relationship being afforded to you, your sacrifice seems costly, like the worth of a rare silver dollar, and it seems you are only going to get about twenty-five cents' worth of deeper relational connection with God. Your sacrifice-to-reward ratio is going to be out of sync with the vow. Don't go there.

If going against your own wants and desires is critical to a rich, transformed spiritual life, you can easily understand why so many modern Christians appear weak and untransformed by their faith. Perhaps our general ignorance of the role and purpose of sacrifice in faith coupled with our culture's general commitment to hedonism helps us understand why the West has come to be called a "post-Christian" culture.

9. Avoid vow-making unless you are prepared to keep your promise. It is possible to get so excited and happy before the Lord that we vow about things we cannot live up to. This qualifies as the "rash" talk and "hasty" promises that Solomon calls the "sacrifice of fools."[33] The Bible is clear that our mouths can be a cause of sin and a source of destruction in our lives.[34] Watch what you say. We are responsible for what we have vowed to do. Deliver on your promise.

It is not a sin to abstain from making promises, but once made, a promise must be kept. If we promise something to God, we must follow through no matter what. A vow to God is extremely serious business.

Words are cheap; actions are what count. Don't fall into the sin of broken promises. God doesn't want us to "talk a good talk" and live in a way that contradicts our words. Instead, we should put feet on our faith. Sinning by breaking a vow is not unpardonable, but sin is always debilitating.

This is just another reason why you and I must be careful about vow-making. We should only vow in areas we know we want to commit to doing when the "wind" of excitement has abandoned our sails and we are stuck out on the ocean of can't-turn-back-now commitment.

If you make a vow to God, you have to keep it. That is the bottom line. There is no other way to look at it. There is no way to soften it or to make it easier to swallow. Once it is out there it is carved in stone. You no longer face your same old life. You are no longer the same old person. You no longer serve yourself. You are defined by your vow.

10. Date your vows before you marry them. Remember that it is important only to vow into things that you have already experienced grace in. You should never try to vow into something because you are hoping it will help you stick to what you think you should be more consistent in. For example, if you have never been one to consistently read your Bible but you feel you should, don't vow to do it right away! That would be premature, and you'll just be setting yourself up for failure.

First, pray about how you view Scripture. What value does it have to you as an individual? Do you believe it is God's word to you? What have you experienced as you've encountered its claims? What do you love about the Bible, and what do you feel uneasy about? Then learn different ways to approach the Scriptures. Most evangelicals are only aware of approaching the Bible by studying it using various study aids (exegetical books, commentaries, study Bibles, preaching and teaching, and so on). But there is another ancient way that is being rediscovered by many moderns. It is the technique referred to as *lecto divina*—a slow, contemplative praying of the Scriptures which enables the Bible, the Word of God, to become a means of union with God. This ancient practice has been kept alive in the Christian monastic tradition for centuries.

The art of *lecto divina* begins with cultivating the ability to listen deeply, to hear, in the words of St. Benedict, "with the ear of our hearts."[35] This is a way to imitate the prophet Elijah, who listened for the still, small voice of God.[36] *Lecto divina* is the practice of gentle listening as an attunement to the presence of God while we read or listen to that special part of God's creation, which are the Scriptures. As we read or pray the Scriptures contemplatively, we listen for the faint murmuring sound of God's voice touching our hearts through his Word. Very cool.

Try approaching the Bible both ways. You may find that one seems to connect you with God more easily than the other—*or* both may do so in different ways. As you focus on the grace that is communicated to your soul, you will find yourself delighting to go to the Scriptures over and over again without ever vowing about it. But if you decide to enter a vow concerning this (or any other area), make sure you have had sufficient time practicing it first. Date it before you marry it. Make sure you love it enough and experience enough grace from it to warrant making it a permanent part of your Christian praxis. Is this really a way you want to give definition to your love for God? And if you do decide you want to vow to it, make it a short-term (six months to one year) rather than lifelong vow. If after a short-term vow you are convinced it is a practice from which you never want to retreat, make a lifelong vow.

11. What do you say when you vow? When you actually make a vow, keep it simple. Solomon wrote concerning vowing, "Let your words be few."[37] When I vowed into the Daily Office, I simply said, "Lord, I vow to participate in the Daily Office until next January." And I wrote it down. As a matter of course, every day I read the vows I have made and reaffirm my commitment to them before the Lord.

You may want to add a little more pomp and circumstance to your vow-making (as we do with marital vows). You could go down by the river or park and take some communion elements with you and recite your vow and receive communion. You could have a few close friends with you or ask your pastor to be a part of it. Remember, this is yours to do or not to do. Do what's most meaningful to you. Make it your own.

12. Who should you tell about your vows? As long as you are not bragging or calling attention to yourself, there is nothing wrong with others knowing about a vow you are making. However, it is completely appropriate to keep it just between you and God as well. I did speak with my wife and those I work with about my Daily Office vow because it affected them—I steal off several times a day to spend time doing my Scripture reading and prayers. I felt like they needed to know what I was sneaking off to do. But there are a couple other areas I have made vows about that no one knows but God. And I like that. It adds a preciousness and a holiness to them for me.

Next, we begin to examine the different kinds of vows that individuals and communities can make.

12. KINDS OF VOWS

Then will I ever sing praise to your name
and fulfill my vows day after day.
—Ps. 61:8

The word "television" literally means seeing something (*vision*) from a distance (*tele*). For many in the West, television has become just that—living life "from a distance." Millions stare at their TV screens night after night, mesmerized by news shows, dramas, comedies, documentaries, romantic and action features that broadcast a mixture of the real, the imaginary, and the exaggerated into their homes and lives. These viewers are living, but they are living secondhand, one step removed from the lives they are watching.

I'm a big fan of the series *24* featuring Keifer Sutherland as super-agent Jack Bauer. *Whoa.* By the time I watch him get shot, stabbed, or tortured, get up and chase a bad guy a few miles on foot, kill three to four people in hand-to-hand combat along the way, catch that bad guy he was chasing and get him back to CTU for interrogation—all in one episode—I'm exhausted. Though I've been sitting the whole time, I feel like

I have worked out, courageously deterred a terrorist from his or her diabolical scheme to hurt the United States, and brought some good old-fashioned justice on several deserving thugs. A busy night indeed. And all done vicariously through my imag- ined-*me*, Jack Bauer, from the privacy of my very own living room. It's me living life "from a distance."

Sadly, this is the way many in the church live out the vision of God for their lives. We want to change the world, but we want to do it with minimum involvement. We want "tele-mis- sion" or "tele-church." I have been pastoring for over twenty- five years, and I have seen how many saints want the church staff to organize programs and outreach initiatives and disciple- ship pathways, not because they want to get involved in them; they just want to feel like they are part of an organization com- mitted to changing the world, which means *they* are changing the world . . . though it's secondhand and one step removed.

What I love about vow-making is that it ensures that everyone in the body of Christ gets their skin in the game. We actually engage in the mission of God by getting off of our blessed assurance and doing something—this is the stuff of real vision, not the "tele" kind.

Vows and Mission

As you enter the arena of vow-making, it is important that you remember you are not just vowing to do just *anything* you want to do—a vow is an "act of generosity toward God."[1] Presumably you must vow into things that matter to God more than to you. This means vows are more than New Year's resolutions that you would make about things that matter to you—things *you* want to change. Vows are not of this sort. They are expressions of love and thanksgiving for actions done by God, not an attempt to improve the quality of your life (though they most likely will). Vows remind us and show God that we have drawn our stakes out of this world and have planted them in the kingdom that is to come. We have fundamentally and ultimately relocated our treasures in heaven.[2] We find the things that communicate his presence and grace, and we vow into them. Vows are a kind of cement that hold us in the expression of love for God.

Michael Frost and Alan Hirsch assert that all Christ-followers need to hold three areas of concern in tension: *communion* (our relationship with Christ), *community* (our relationship with one another in the believing community), and *commission* (our relationship to the world and the mission God has given us to reach them with the truth of Christ).[3] They warn that it is foolish to focus on any *one* area at the expense of the rest, and that a "balanced" approach placing equal importance on all three areas is what God desires for all of us. Any vow worth considering will fall within one of these three broad areas.

Vows of Communion

Vows of Communion are any vows that have as their primary end a more intimate relationship with God. Most vows fit in here. These are the vows that are jammed with various classic spiritual disciplines, such as those of *abstinence* (solitude, silence, fasting, frugality, chastity, secrecy, sacrifice) or those of *engagement* (study, worship, celebration, service, prayer, fellowship, confession, submission).[4] We do these spiritual activities in the vowing context because the whole point of the vow is to get caught up in an infatuation with the holy. We do them because we have a burning passion for a living relationship with God. The possibilities are endless, but let's address a few possible vows.

Examples of Vows of Communion

Vows of Examination. This kind of vow could involve everything from committing to going to a counselor to discover exactly *what* is contributing to your failure in some area of your life (marriage, career, parenting, and so on), to fasting for a season to ask God to reveal what is "triggering" some pattern of sin you seem to bumble into with a degree of regularity, to looking for and taking assessment tests to discover your personality, emotional, or motivational strengths and weaknesses, to joining a small group focused on principles of "examen" (such as the RENOVARÉ spiritual formation groups discussed below).

This is the world of Spirit-led self-examination. But facing yourself is a scary enterprise. Most of us live in denial because we can't bear the truth about ourselves. The comic-strip character Pogo put it so aptly, "We have met the enemy, and it is us." Jesus said, "I have much more to say to you, more than you can now bear."[4] He knows we have a hard time facing the mirror. I think if God told us everything we are doing wrong, we'd quit; we'd be too discouraged to push on.

The good news is God knows us completely and is still wildly and recklessly in love with us *just as we are.* J. I. Packer writes, "There is tremendous relief in knowing that his love to me is utterly realistic, based at every point on prior knowledge of the worst about me, so that no discovery now can disillusion him about me, in the way I am so often disillusioned about myself."[5]

Virginia Lively tells of a vision she once had of Jesus Christ that gives us a snapshot of this kind of love. She writes, "[The] thing that struck me was his utter lack of condemnation. I realized at once that he knew me down to my very marrow. He knew all the stupid, cruel, silly things I had ever done. But I also realized that none of these things—nothing I could ever do—would alter the absolute caring, the unconditional love that I saw in his eyes. I could not grasp it! It was too immense a fact. I felt that if I gazed at him for a thousand years, I still could not realize the enormity of that love."[6]

I have no idea why God loves us like this, but he does. God is just like that. This is the beauty of his love and grace. When this truth becomes real, there is no more fear of abandonment. In fact, this "perfect love drives out fear."[7] We don't have to be afraid anymore. Dare to explore the Vow of Examination to really get to know yourself. The psalmist plunges into this when he cries out, "Search me, O God, and know my heart; test me and know my anxious thoughts. See if there is any offensive way in me, and lead me in the way everlasting."[8]

Vows of Development

Another kind of communion vow is a vow of development. This vow would address the fact that we must grow in our faith intentionally. True, God will love us if we don't, but I want to. I want to because it impacts everything else. Paul said, "Godliness has value for all things, holding promise for both the present life and the life to come."[9] But spiritual growth requires time spent with God in prayer. There are just some things that cannot be communicated until you spend time, sometimes excruciatingly boring times, shut away trying to talk with God. Fasting helps; it's like *super*-prayer, but you need to learn to reinterpret your natural hunger as a "hunger" for God. Studying the Scriptures is critical; you can only know God by what he says about himself, not what you feel like that day. Listening to life-giving preaching via going to church or listening to podcasts from ministers who seem to charge your soul is simple and beneficial. Learning to "Sabbath," where you actually take a day off to refresh and restore and enjoy some recreation, which, incidentally, is re-*creation*. Find the things that throw you most wholly on God—things that make you *grow*, and vow into them.

The RENOVARÉ spiritual formation groups are a great resource for participating in a vow of development (www.renovare.org). Founded by Richard Foster, RENOVARÉ (a Latin word meaning "to renew") is a system of small groups committed to working through (with questions of "examen" and corporate prayer) the six traditional streams of the Christian faith, which they describe as: Contemplative: The Prayer-Filled Life; Holiness: The Virtuous Life; Charismatic: The Spirit-Empowered Life; Social Justice: The Compassionate Life; Evangelical: The Word-Centered Life; and Incarnational: The Sacramental Life.

Members of a RENOVARÉ spiritual formation group focus on these six streams by reading devotional materials and Scripture, encouraging each other to participate in the common disciplines, and using the "Questions of Examen," which give accountability to their discipleship efforts. Their motto is the Latin phrase *Credo Ergo Ado*—I believe, therefore I do. Each person commits (vows) to the process and attends the weekly small group meetings, which are characterized by grace, mercy, love, and support. Foster writes, "God today is calling his children to grow up. Perpetual spiritual infancy does not please

God nor does it honor Christ. RENOVARÉ has come into being in response to this new (yet old) call of God for maturity. We seek to set forth a practical strategy for spiritual growth that is for all who follow Christ. It is a strategy that we believe God is using to bring people everywhere 'To grow up in every way into him who is the head, into Christ' (Eph. 4:15)."[10]

My favorite of the Vows of Development is the Daily Office. "Office" as a word comes into modern usage from the Latin word *opus*, or "work." For most of us the word makes us think of a place rather than an activity (unless you think of someone running for a public "office"). It was Saint Benedict who first said, "*Orare est laborare, laborare est orare.*" "To pray is to work, to work is to pray." Hence, the Daily Office is referring to the "work" of the believer.

From the beginning of Christianity believers have seen prayer and meditation as the divine work we are invited to participate in. These are prayers and praise offered as a sweet-smelling sacrifice of thanksgiving and faith to God—part of what constitutes the priesthood of the believer. Historically the Daily Office focuses on praying portions of the Psalms, the Our Father, prayers of petition, moments of silent reflection, recitation of creeds, general Bible passages, and devotional reading covering broader spiritual formation themes and ideas. (See Appendix B for a Daily Office sampler.)

The positive impact of this practice on my soul cannot be overstated. As I have said, grace is most powerfully communicated to me through meditation and prayer, so this feels like a shot of adrenaline to my soul. Before I entered a vow of practicing the Daily Office, I would enjoy a devotional time in Scripture and prayer in the mornings. And I loved it. I usually could live on that fresh wind of the Holy Spirit till mid- to late morning . . . then the day would kick in and I'd be left with only the faint memory of devotion. By late afternoon or evening I usually found myself starting to "stink" spiritually—especially if my day was a real workout.

The Daily Office has become a frequent "grace shower" for me. But I don't wait till I stink to take a shower. The Daily Office is an odor-prevention strategy. I usually do an office after I wake in the morning, then again at noon, mid-afternoon, after dinner, and right before I go to bed. (I've even started doing one around 3:00 AM and it's been a kick!). I have found that when the "glory" of the moment passes I begin to anticipate the next office without effort. When I feel myself being drawn into impatience or have an inappropriate imagination, I almost unconsciously draw back in view of the fact that I'm going to be talking with God very soon.

Whenever you take an antibiotic, the doctor usually prescribes that the pills be taken two to four times a day. If you ask why, she will tell you it's because she wants the strength of the medication to be at a constant level in your system throughout the day—not just to spike at one point in the day. This holds true for God's power and presence in your life. I think God wants you to be full of his joy and peace and kindness throughout the day, not just for an hour or two after a morning devotion or a Sunday service. I think he wants you to be jammed with spiritual energy as you walk throughout your whole day. The result will be that you will have little room for your lower nature to blossom. You will find that the overall tenor of your soul will greatly improve as you practice the Daily Office—that's why I have vowed into it.

Vows of Community

Vows of Community are any vows that have as their primary end a more intimate relationship with God but are done in the company of others. There are times when it is completely appropriate to enter a vow as a group. As I mentioned earlier, the community I am a part of decided to participate in corporate fasting. It was an amazing experience to enter a vow with others. Last fall we did another corporate vow where about a hundred of us spent a month experimenting with the classic disciplines, especially the ones we were less familiar with.

Corporate vowing affords us accountability and empowerment simply because we are doing it together. From health clubs to dieting organizations, we all recognize the power in reaching goals and committing to new paths together. And the presence of accountability and encouragement from others helps us experience transformation. This is no less true for developing spiritually. Grace, it turns out, is communicated to us both individually and corporately. That would mean that faith is as corporate as it is individual.

Humans are by nature individual and communal beings. To feel actualized, we must find expression both as individuals and within the context of community. The idea of communal expression is most critical within the dimension of faith. We are not supposed to live out faith on our own. Sadly, in the evangelical tradition there is little discussion about or awareness of the catholicity of faith. We generally assume we are supposed to live out faith on our own. James Sanders suggests that many in our culture "think of religion as a personal matter and concern, something between them as individuals and God."[11] Though few evangelicals would hold to the idea that community is

155

inconsequential, our view of community is quite pale. Perhaps that is because individual faith has been too radicalized. Though I feel indebted to my heritage for many good things as an evangelical, the absence of a robust communal dimension of faith is, more often than not, tragic.

In addition, one could argue that the values present in Western culture (such as materialism, rabid individualism, commercialism, and so on) further wound the significance we place on community. Our technological advances tend to isolate us further (with indoor plumbing, we no longer draw together at the community well, and washing machines keep us from chatting down by the river).

Leo Buscalia challenges us with what he witnessed while touring in the Far East:

> When the Monsoons come, the great rains wash away all their houses and take away everything they have. Then these people get on communal rafts, several families living together. The rains come, the rafts rise, and they go on living, but now communally. I thought, wouldn't that be beautiful, if six months out of every year some of us could live together? I can see you thinking—Who wants to live with my neighbor? But maybe it would be a beautiful thing to live with a neighbor and to find out what it is again to be dependent upon people and how beautiful it is to be able to say to someone, "I need you." We think to be a grownup we must be independent and not need anyone. And that's why we're all dying of loneliness.[12]

Even the pagan Aristotle, in discussing ethics, asserted that community is crucial. He claimed that if "each man lives as he pleases" he lives "as the Cyclopes do."[13] The mythical Cyclopes were mean, destructive beings. I fear that our lack of true community and intimacy and our rabid individuality have made the typical Western evangelical church monstrous.

The power of community means we are not solitary prophets. Our insights are shared and we challenge each other with them together. We learn interdependence. There is both glory and brokenness in life; we are to share in both. Paul wrote concerning community, "If one member suffers, all the parts [share] the suffering; if one member is honored, all the members [share in] the enjoyment of it."[14] Vowing can be used to express faith in both individual and corporate ways. Though we must champion and encourage the personal journey of faith, we need to mitigate radical individualism through a robust dimension of communal faith.

Examples of Vows of Community

From birth to death, life is full of challenges and seasons chock-full of issues that must be successfully navigated for one to live a fully human life. Corporate vow-making can help individuals make those transitions with more grace and ease. From learning how to work through obedience, work, relationships, faith, sexuality, and so on, to changing your focus and reinventing yourself in order to meet the changing needs which pop up in the various stages of life—being single, becoming young parents, experiencing the "empty-nest," retirement, aging, and facing death—finding others who are going through similar transitions and vowing into grace together to address and share the burden and glory God gives is a gift indeed.

Imagine a group of twenty-something men vowing into a

community for a period of one year. During this time they live together, vow into celibacy (they're going to refrain from dating), chastity (they are going to redirect their sexual passion), and service (they are going to take on some missional project, like making friends with fatherless kids in the church or nearby apartment complex). They have a rich culture of prayer, solitude, confession, submission, and so on, and, since they have vowed into this, they cannot retreat from working through the disruptive, relational things that would make most guys quit.

Imagine a group of young mothers who meet with a couple of empty-nested moms for a series of lessons dealing with the disturbances that a child entering an existing family unit creates: time schedules overhauled, new rules because a new person is in the house, curtailed activities common to the couple before arrival of the baby, sexual and intimacy conflicts that can erupt between the couple, and so on. The group vows into participation, honesty, and privacy as they look for God to move in their midst while they dig into the material and love each other recklessly.

The possibilities for community vow-making are only limited by the imagination.

A Community of Equals

There is something about entering into vows together that reaffirms the reality that we are part of a community of equals. Paul wrote,

> But I also want you to think about how this keeps your significance from getting blown up into self-importance. For no matter how significant you are, it is only because of what you

are a part of. An enormous eye or a gigantic hand wouldn't be a body, but a monster. What we have is one body with many parts, each its proper size and in its proper place. No part is important on its own. Can you imagine Eye telling Hand, "Get lost; I don't need you"? The way God designed our bodies is a model for understanding our lives together as a church: every part dependent on every other part.[15]

My first job out of high school was at a fast-food restaurant. I was the "fry guy." It didn't take me long to discover that the fry guy was also the one who did all the heavy work in the place. It was almost like a hazing ritual. I was responsible for all the bad jobs: mopping the slimy floor in the kitchen, pulling out the heavy boxes from the freezer, filtering the grease from the fries, and so on. It was part of the job description for the "fry guy"—the one who was *always* the new guy. The seasoned vets were the upperclassmen. They had paid their dues. They got to do the sexy stuff: wait on customers, flip burgers, laugh and joke and bark orders at the "fry guy."

On some level, the church works like this. The new converts are the fry guys or gals. It's on their shoulders to learn how to serve the Lord, to learn the Scriptures, to change their lifestyles to more closely represent those of us who have been on the Way longer than they have—to look like us, act like us, talk like us, pretend to be us . . . all in the name of discipleship, of course. Those of us who have been around for a while have already paid our dues. We used to grow, but no longer—we are now the "grown," the "mature." We're the "fathers" and the "rabbis." And we get to do the sexy stuff like make sure the others respect, awe, and adore us. That's what leadership is . . . right?

But what if there is a kind of work that we are *all* supposed to be doing, an engagement of faith from which we never graduate? What if vow-making is an example of that kind of work—where each of us looks for the things that communicate grace to our souls and we vow into those areas . . . together? What if spiritual life is more like the ongoing battle of staying in shape physically than the static accomplishment of getting a degree in school? If that is true, on one level the Christian life would be like a marathon and we would all need to stay in shape together as marathon runners—young and old, novice and expert. We would be a "community of equals."

Vows of Commission

Paul said, "Those who have trusted in God may be careful to devote themselves to doing what is good. These things are excellent and profitable for everyone."[16] As we pointed out in Chapter 1, the word "devote" is actually derived from the word "vow." Promising to do "good," "excellent," and "profitable" works vis-à-vis a vow is completely appropriate—these constitute the "Vows of Commission." Vows of Commission would include commitments to participate in evangelism, church work, social justice programs, ministry to the sick and dying, educational programs, and so on.

Vows of Commission are promises to engage in good works, not works that are attempts to secure salvation—those would be "dead works." We engage in "good works" because we have been touched and salvaged in this world by God. Paul claimed that when we discover that Jesus "gave himself for us to redeem us from all wickedness and to purify for himself a people that are his very own," we become "eager to do what is good."[17] Personal and corporate vows ensure we push past the mere *intention* of eagerness into *action*.

In the spring of 2007 a great movie entitled *Amazing Grace* was released based on the true story of William Wilberforce's life. Wilberforce and a group of friends gathered together at Clapham, South London, in the late 1700s and early 1800s to commit to a common goal of changing the world. This little group, known as the Clapham Sect, consisted of business people, clergymen, politicians, and a playwright. The most famous among them was Wilberforce, who was a Member of Parliament.

Wilberforce had an amazing conversion experience at age twenty-six and considered resigning from politics to go into the ministry. It was John Newton (who was a former slave-trader and author of the hymn "Amazing Grace") who convinced him that God was the one who had put him in Parliament and that he should fight against the abolition of slavery. The group regularly met in the home of a wealthy banker to scheme about changing society and evangelizing the world. They not only fought slavery but worked to improve the conditions for workers, established several missionary societies, started schools, worked to ban bull-fighting, and secured permission for missionaries to go to India. But it all came through much work, personal financial cost, and years lived under the threat of assassination by the slave lobby. Wilberforce actually had a nervous breakdown and nearly died. But eventually the Clapham Sect achieved their lifelong dream of the emancipation of slaves as British citizens. A small group of individuals vowing into a deep friendship and some common goals was able to change the whole world for Jesus Christ.

The World of "Eager" Intentions

I have a friend who recently told me that a few months ago he and six other dads were gathered around the TV watching a football game. A conversation erupted about their boys (each of them had a son around the age of fifteen). My friend said they all got stoked about the idea of doing four major father-son events a year together as a group. They even talked about what those events would look like and how they would use their time together to inculcate values and issues of faith into their boys. They left the game that night eager and expectant.

But as the weeks passed, my friend, who was the one responsible to set up the first event, found himself putting the trip planning on the back burner—life has a way of "back-burnering" the best intentions. By the time he got back to the other men, about eight weeks had passed. By then all the emotion of that night had been forgotten, and he could only get *one* of the dads to commit to anything.

Didn't the rest of the dads care? Of course they did. Don't they love their boys enough to do it? Yes, they love their boys enough. But here's the problem. We're fooled by *intention*. We judge other people by their actions—what they do or don't do—but we tend to judge ourselves by our intentions. I can't tell you how many times my wife has asked me to do something (like clean the garage) and I intended to do it. But an unexpected phone call or friend stopped by and it didn't happen. I think, *No big deal*, because I *intended* to do it.

Gail, on the other hand, only sees that something she has asked me to do goes undone. She doesn't know my intentions, so she's disappointed in me. The bottom line is that intentions really don't mean *anything*. The garage is still dirty. Vow-making is a cure for this. If something is worth intending, it is worth doing. Why do vows help? Because vows preempt the fickle will that goes all topsy-turvy and inconsistent whenever something pressing, unexpected, or more fun shows up. Vows are commitments from which there is no retreat.

The Order of the Mustard Seed

In his book *The Vision and the Vow*, Pete Grieg explores the fascinating vow of the eighteenth-century count Ludwig Nicklaus von Zinzendorf and a few of his friends. They called themselves the Honourable Order of the Mustard Seed. Each of the members wore a ring with the inscribed motto "None live for themselves," and they vowed to be true to Christ, to be kind to people, and to take the gospel of Christ to the nations.[18]

It all began with Zinzendorf and five of his friends in high school. They had a hand in a revival that swept through their school and felt that God wanted to use them as a team. After they all went in different directions to college, they stayed connected via letters. Then in the spring of 1718, they arranged a meeting where they formally took vows that brought the Order into being. This small group of men, who had vowed into keeping each other at the task of being true to Christ, kind to people, and spreading the gospel, did everything from establishing mission endeavors to spurning significant revivals. They changed the world in which they lived, leaving it better than they found it. This is the power of vow-making.

When we act, the world is changed and we become "splendors" for God. Vows of Communion, Vows of Community, and Vows of Commission are all about action. C. S. Lewis once said, "There are no ordinary people. You have never met a mere mortal. Nations, cultures, arts, civilizations—these are mortal and their life is to ours as a gnat. But it is immortals whom we joke with, work with, marry, snub, and exploit—immortal horrors or everlasting splendors."[19] Our choices determine whether we are "horrors" or "splendors." Which do you want to be?

13. Vow-making Brings Influence

For you have heard my vows, O God; you have given me
the heritage of those who fear your name.
—Ps. 61:5

I think God is inviting the twenty-first-century church to love him more deeply. The ancient Latin phrase *extremis malis extrema remedia*, loosely translated, is "Desperate times call for desperate measures." I think every apprentice of Jesus Christ would agree that there is much desperation in our world. There are many challenges we must face in our postmodern context: indifference, continuing de-Christianization, fanaticism, consumerism, stress, and individualism, to name a few. But hope overcomes all this; it pushes beyond these limits.

Nevertheless, there are elements that are still frightening, struggles that must be navigated and appropriately addressed. Yet, there is a hope to his calling us. God's call means he is not finished here. Jesus said the kingdom of God is something that one should "seize it by force [as a precious prize—a share in the heavenly kingdom is sought with most ardent zeal and intense exertion]."[1] We need special wisdom and revelation to catch the import of that, and I *want* to catch the import of that. I want to "live a life worthy of the Lord" and so "please him in every way: bearing fruit in every good work."[2]

The Way Things Are

I, like so many, feel great ambivalence about the church—there are parts of church life I love and parts I'm confused about. It's not that I want to leave the church, but in a way it feels as if the church has left me. There is little transformation, little evidence that we are all that different from those in our culture without faith. We sin, divorce, hate, and get in trouble as often as everyone else—the values of our Christ-less culture are being inculcated into our thinking and ways of living. Instead of being "in" the world and not "of" it[3] as Jesus prayed, we are firmly "of" it.

Some respond to this by getting meaner or by establishing harsher rules that end up creating the haves and the have nots, the spiritual and the carnal, the elite and the common. But these kinds of distinctions, while motivating to some, only feed our lower nature with the fodder of dissensions and factions, which are really anti-Christ in nature.[4]

Others respond with the notion that we will only be safe if we retreat into some kind of "gated community" of programs and buildings. Then we are to do everything we can to get folks to come into the safety of *us*. It's a kind of build-it-and-they-will-come strategy. Howard Snyder claims, "The gospel says 'Go,' but our church buildings say, 'Stay.' The gospel says, 'Seek the lost,' but our churches say, 'Let the lost seek the church.'"[5] Snyder goes on to say that without realizing it, this kind of isolation theology has created a litany of problems in the church, including immobility, inflexibility, a lack of true community or fellowship, pride, and some rigid class distinctions. There have been times in recent years where I started to believe in organizational euthanasia—I wanted to pull the plug on how we do church.

The problem is that we tend to give more credence to institutionalizing church life than to the church herself—to the *people*. When we institutionalize church life—make it all about buildings and programs, along with funding and staffing those things—instead of making it about the unfolding stories of the people who make her up, we lose our corporate soul. The institution is always concerned about who isn't "here" and how to get them "here" and how to use the resources of those sitting in the pews to get them "here." The facilitation of personal gifts and charisms of the individuals already sitting "here" remain untapped for mission. Instead, church leaders disseminate vision to the people who are expected to be mere receivers of vision just because they are the leader's followers. But aren't leaders responsible to unearth the dreams and visions of those who are *in the pews*—to be a kind of midwife committed to helping give birth to the unique dreams of God lying in the soul of every believer they are responsible for? Aren't leaders to be like parents who give vocabulary, legitimacy, and direction to the dreams of their children? I think so. Sadly, though, the only opportunity afforded to those who sit in our churches is for them to give money and volunteer for some leader-initiated program. And one only needs to have a pulse to qualify for giving or volunteerism; you don't need to have a soul.

I know this sounds bleak, but I am not a fatalist. Though I think we are in crisis, there *are* signs of life and hope in the church. There is much right in her. I'm hoping that discussions like this one about vow-making can add more hope. The Chinese term for "crisis" (*wei-ji*) speaks of both danger and opportunity. This means that crisis is really a dimension of transformation. And most of us know deep in our souls that we cannot play games—there is too much at stake. We must have authentic transformation.

The Way Things Ought to Be

The church is to be a band of people who are authentically transformed. This is why I have such enthusiasm about vow-making. Vows facilitate transformation. Vows tie us to the reality of eternal things in a whole new way—giving us hope for a brand new future. Vows are simply one's own love, transformed and directed toward God and the cause of his kingdom. And they are sweet. By vowing we establish a new framework that facilitates an openness to God where the Spirit of God is active and present in one's life. We know he is active whether one vows or not, but vowing is a commitment to attend to his presence and activity, to ensure the activity is not ignored nor missed.

I believe participating in vow-making invites God's action into our history. Through vows we nail our lives to his rule. It is important to remember that we have a penchant to push away from God's rule and to attach our desires to lesser things. In fact, doing so is the reality and sign of our human fallenness—it's one of the *only* things we do consistently well. The energy we have for God gets shifted and attached to other things: goods, ideals, work, relationships, and so on. We attach our desire for God to things that are not God.

Attaching our energy to other things is *addiction*. If you hold up a picture against the wall, you can move it around at will. But if you nail it there, it hangs without needing or seeking your permission. If we are not very careful, the energies we could use for God become attached to other things, "addicted" to things other than God. That's when we lose freedom and control over our energy. Addictions seize our desires (we're nailed), leaving less and less desire available for love of God, people, or any other worthwhile pursuits. The Bible refers to this kind of dynamic as *idolatry*. Idolatry is all about trying to fulfill the human longing for God with something other than God.

As a result, we find ourselves in a state of compulsion or obsession. We are compelled to give energy to things that are not our true desires. Sadly, this kind of enslaved living is reinforced in a consumer society like ours. Through the power of suggestion and mass advertising, our desire gets attached to things we don't even need or want. Society tells us that our sense of self is to be grounded in things, and since we want to belong, we succumb to its siren song. But society never tells us the whole truth—that things will never give us our true identity.

That doesn't mean we don't use things and trust God for things. We do. There is nothing wrong with things, and God does promise to be our Provider,[6] but we don't just want our possessions to define who we are. One Christian leader said it best,

It is not wrong to want to live better; what is wrong is a style of life which is presumed to be better when it is directed toward "having" rather than "being" and which wants to have more not in order to be more, but in order to spend life in enjoyment as an end in itself.[7]

"Being" is a call to *action,* not just to *believing.* The hard truth is that people in our culture are not interested in what we believe. However, they *are* interested in beliefs that have actually changed us. They want to know whether we believe what we believe in order to belong to a certain group or if our beliefs actually change the way in which we live. Do they alter our story? Paul claimed the gospel was designed to rewrite a person's life. He said, "Your very lives are a letter that anyone can read by just looking at you. Christ himself wrote it—not with ink, but with God's living Spirit; not chiseled into stone, but carved into human lives—and we publish it."[8] Few things capture us like people stories. We are fascinated by real life and ordinary people—perhaps because we recognize that each of our lives is jammed with similar struggles and ironies, and stories of transformation strike us; they give us hope.

Authentically transformed people are those who live in ways that contradict the *vox populi*—the general population. Ours is a culture that has lost track of values beyond utilitarianism—if a choice we make gets us what we want, we assume it must be right. We overcome this by living differently—radically by some standards. In contradistinction to a life committed to selfdom, things like obedience, sacrifice, simplicity, humility, holiness, kindness, patience, goodness, self-control, and so on, mark our lives. It is this kind of living that creates a question in the minds and lives of those within our sphere—we begin to influence others.

Vow-making is both personally transformational and political. Our union with the person of God never just takes place in our hearts or personal space, it influences situations, community, family, friendships, civic work—everything. Faith is pushed out of the domain of thought. Our choices plunge us into real life and all the suffering and contradictions that occur there, while we remain steady in our devotion. This is a quest for influence.

This is how the typical mom with three kids still in diapers can influence the world. This is how the high-school student, who is still trying to discover who she is and where she fits in the world, can influence others for Jesus. This is how the retired person struggling with health issues or caring for an elderly parent changes the world. The apostle Peter claimed that when we live our lives in a way that shows we have "set apart Christ as Lord" in our hearts, we will create a question in the minds of others. Peter contends that the role of the believer is to "always be prepared to give an answer" to the emerging questions from those who observe our lives.[9] Somehow, as we intentionally "set apart Christ as Lord" in our hearts (which is the point of vow-making), we start looking different; our story changes. We become marked with "bright spots" (joy, peace, kindness, patience, hope, and so on). These bright spots create a question inside those who live in our proximity. When the question comes, Peter says we are to answer. I suggest that answering the question our lives create is the secret to changing the world around us.

It's not that we are perfect or that we have all the answers for all the problems of the world. But we refuse to let our uncertainties paralyze us, and we are willing to live in a way that critiques society and the church, all the while admitting our own inadequacies and contradictions. And though we seem small in the overall scheme of things, we constantly embrace the hope that God loves to use small things to change the world—we can be a part of building a different, better world.

Political Power or Personal Influence?

When we vow into living consistently, our internal renewal is pushed out into the public sphere. This gives us a voice in the world in which we live. The past forty years have been a bit of a roller-coaster ride for the American evangelical church in this regard. For too long evangelicals sequestered religion to the domain of private piety, which limited faith to personal matters—our faith needed to go public. And we longed to make it public. Wanting to influence the public sphere was the right idea; it's how we tried that ended up (in my estimation) hurting the cause of Christ. Instead of emerging into the public forum as transformed, engaging individuals, we ended up leaping with reckless abandon in rallying support for political agendas—eventually becoming convinced that God was a Republican and trying to keep as many televangelists and radio preachers in the media as we could. We thought they were invading the culture with the claims of Christ. It turns out for the most part they were confusing the culture more than helping it.

Our approach to establish faith vis-à-vis political, economic, and social pressure failed. However, God still wants us to establish faith in the public sphere; we must keep dancing between both the religious-philosophical and political dimensions, and we must learn to do it well. That is part of our mission. However, we must rethink how we engage in the public sphere. I suggest we recalibrate our "public-ness" in pursuit of influence more than power.

Gail and I are now parents of four adult children. We used to have power over them; now we have no real "power," but we do have *influence*. Truth be told, we like influencing better than powering. It lends itself more to respect for and faith in our kids and is less centered on us. We like nurturing and supporting more than we liked bossing and ruling. I think this can carry into reimagining the public role of the church.

Not long before her death I heard that Mother Teresa had spoken at one of the most prestigious Ivy League schools in the Northeast. I had read how evangelical and conservative leaders had been badgered with protests, catcalls, and disruptions when they spoke at those bastions of liberalism, and I was completely surprised and delighted to hear how warmly and respectfully they received Mother Teresa. I think the reason they did is because she is a symbol of powerlessness. She wasn't after political, intellectual, or social currency when she spoke (as most other leaders are); she simply told her story and asked them to consider the claims of Christ to protect life and care for the hurting and dying. During the whole ninety-minute speech the room was silent enough to hear a pin drop, and she was met with a standing ovation at the end.

It turns out that power doesn't always win in the end—someone will always end up being more powerful than you—but influence always wins. I think the church in the West should seek to be powerless. We must give up on the quest for power and simply embrace a sacrificial way of living that garners respect and the ear of outsiders who will consider the message of hope we have been entrusted with.

It wasn't until the third or fourth centuries that the Christian church got a taste for power. Up until that point Christianity was about living a certain way—in fact, it was referred to as "the Way."[10] Buildings, hierarchy, polity, political clout, and the like were just not embraced or sought for—living differently, living prophetically as a critique to the misplaced values and beliefs of Christless culture was.

But living prophetically is messy and difficult for leaders to control—it rests too securely in the domain of personal choice and cannot be mandated or coerced. Leaders found it much easier to pool political clout and amass financial strength in the hopes of ensuring (even forcing?) people to act righteously. The problem is that externally coerced righteousness doesn't stick. We may be able to get people to "sit down" on the outside, but they will be "standing up" on the inside.

Though God is completely interested in his kingdom being established in this world, he has never been interested in doing it through broken human systems (political, social, economic, and so on). God is simply not impressed with earthly power structures: "Surely the nations are like a drop in a bucket; they are regarded as dust on the scales. . . . Before him all the nations are as nothing; they are regarded by him as worthless and less than nothing."[11]

Scripture tells us that "the devil took [Jesus] to a very high mountain and showed him all the kingdoms of the world and their splendor. 'All this I will give you,' he said, 'if you will bow down and worship me.'"[12] Presumably it was the devil's to give. Jesus was not into kingdoms or splendor—at least not the kind found here on this planet. He said, "My kingdom is not of this world." His followers tried to force him to rebel against Rome and declare himself king—they figured he had the supernatural powers to pull it off.[13] But he refused. In truth, God sees the political, economic, military, and social powers of this world (and their ilk) as "worthless"—mere pantomimes of a future kingdom to come.

A Martyr-People

Did you ever wonder why the church historically has been persecuted and often martyred? Was it just because they preached "getting ready for eternity" or because they were promoting some kind of otherworldly, existential salvation experience? Why would the crazy dictators of the world, like Nero, who slaughtered Christians by the thousands, care about that? Why are the communities that embody the gospel hunted down and killed as they are today?

What is so threatening about the gospel? Was it the promise of "life after death" or was it that the events of Jesus's life, death, and resurrection and the story that those events carry forward into the present, really do make sense of life in a way that is anti-Caesar, anti-worldly. The threat of being a Christ-follower lies in the fact that aligning one's self to the Christ-story makes one belong to a people among whom God is present "to will and to act according to his good purpose."[14] But his action is not just *in* the believing person, but pushes *through* them to the world. Dangerous indeed.

Persecution sprang from the Christians' claim that "God

has made this Jesus, whom you crucified, both Lord and Christ."[15] That is, he is the Messiah and hence the world's true Lord,[16] and the people that are thus gathered around him are members of the *real* kingdom, of which the Roman kingdom is merely a parody. It is among the God-followers that the meaning of human history is embedded, and it is in their midst that the powers of the coming age are dawning as they witness the resurrection of Christ in the way they live and the way they die. The church is the creation of a people who embody an alternative vision of reality and an alternative value system, who testify to the life, death, resurrection, and ascension of Jesus by being the church, by doing life together. They are an entirely new creation, an emblem of what humanity was always supposed to be, and as such, they unmask the fraudulent and thus draw persecution on themselves.

In our final chapter, let's look at how vow-making helps us influence and survive within a Christ-less culture.

14. Vows: Survival 101

A vow of separation to the LORD.
Num. 6:2

It is evident that the church is walking into a dark night of deep cultural displacement. Our old hegemonies—the ways we influenced the world—are passing away. The old symbols of safety—big church buildings, political power, a *Leave It to Beaver* culture, and so on—are becoming more and more a thing of the past. What is needed in these coming days is a prophetic people, tethered to the vision of the kingdom of God through lively confession and prophetic praxis—a vow-rich people. By so living, we do a couple of things: 1) we show that the kingdoms of our world are less than they think they are— we "judge" them; and 2) we embody our salvation in real time in real circumstances—we offer "salvation" to the kingdoms of the world. We need to be, as Paul puts it in Philippians, a *politeuma*—a robust, lively "colony of heaven" situated right smack in the middle of the chaos of pagan culture.

Remember it was Jesus who cried, "I will build my church,

and the gates of Hades will not overcome it."[1] Notice *who* is supposed to be "gated" in Jesus's view. The church is not supposed to be inside a gated fortress . . . "holding on" till Jesus comes. We're supposed to be attacking the dark forces. God doesn't abandon cultures. He doesn't want us enclaved into gated Christian communities waiting for the return of his Son. He wants us to bring his salvation to the ends of the earth as his faithful few in order to "judge" and "save" cultures.

This means we are going to need to be able to excel and succeed in the middle of corrupt systems without being overly critical of those systems or sucked into their corruption. The Christian faith has a built-in tension between belonging to God no matter the cost while incarnating him in this world— bringing him to the world by being his eyes, ears, hands, and feet. To do this the Christ-follower must accept the world and transcend it at the same time; proclaim his or her accord with the world and his or her independence from it in the same breath. We must move toward the world without making it our "center," yet, go beyond it without rejecting it. Tension.

This means we must find the grace to sustain goodness. Goodness is one of the fruit of the Holy Spirit in our lives that convicts us that a basic holiness permeates all things and all people. It's not that we are unaware of the presence of evil by embracing some silly kind of Pollyanna naiveté. It is that we choose to look past it. And we do so because we recognize that God has designed a world where we can "overcome evil with good."[2] We don't have to be freaked out about evil. But that is easier said than done—especially when you still feel the slap of injustice stinging your face. Turning the other cheek—or responding from your "healthy side"—is very hard to do.[3]

False Peace

Most people in the Western church cultivate a false peace by retreating into isolationist, protectionist cultural enclaves rather than attempting to fight and bring transformation to the culture we live in. But when you examine Jesus, the early church, or many of the ancient Jewish God-followers, they all pursued a bold engagement with the cultures they lived within.

Consider those who experienced Babylonian exile in the Old Testament. This was one of the most painful, displacing moments of Israel's history. The sacred temple (representing God's presence and power) had been desecrated and burned to the ground; the centuries-old foundations of the holy city Jerusalem had been destroyed; they were living in a foreign land and being forced to embrace *its* culture and religious systems.

Here is where the psalmist lamented,

> By the rivers of Babylon we sat and wept when we remembered Zion. There on the poplars we hung our harps, for there our captors asked us for songs, our tormentors demanded songs of joy; they said, "Sing us one of the songs of Zion!" How can we sing the songs of the LORD while in a foreign land?[4]

But it is here in this Babylonian hell-hole that we see God's people learning to be God's people in a whole new way—struggling to ward off despair by boldly imagining what it might mean to be God's people without all the symbols of stability from their past: the land, the monarchy, the walls of the city, the temple, their festivals, and so on. Jeremiah, Ezekiel, Daniel, and

Esther all come to mind here. And what we find in the majority of these lives is something very surprising: the people of God become, in a sense, true bearers of the culture that they inhabit, the experts of those cultures—not because they forgot they were the people of God, but rather *because they were the people of God*. What kept them pure in the process was their absolute commitment (a robust vowing tradition) to staying tethered to the practice of their faith (worship, prayer, fasting, and so on), which exposed the pale horror of what was pagan and dehumanizing about the cultures they inhabited. In other words, they both preserved and critiqued the cultures they inhabited—they upheld *and* subverted those cultures at the same time! In a very real way these saints both "judged and saved" the cultures they inhabited.

Daniel and his friends are perhaps the best example of this. When he and his comrades are commissioned for service in the royal court of Babylon, they make the famous decision "not to defile themselves" with the royal food and wine (a vow involving fasting and prayer). And they "gave them vegetables instead."[5] Over time these boys were found to be "healthier and better nourished than any of the young men who ate the royal food."[6]

Imagine these growing teenage boys choosing water and vegetables over the ancient counterpart of Big Macs, fries, and a Coke. This had to mess with them, but that is precisely the point. By vowing themselves into this practice, the hunger served as a constant alarm reminding them that they did not belong to this culture and, though they needed to master its mores and values, they couldn't compromise their own. The fasting served as a mooring rope to help them be "in" the Babylonian culture without being "of" it.

They were not commanded to do this, but they did it. They did it as an act of generosity to God—as a corporate vow. And their vow helped to sustain a rhythm of grace that made serving God in the midst of a corrupt Babylonian world possible. Daniel even participated in a vow similar to the Daily Office by committing to finding a place of solitude three times a day for prayer and meditation.[7]

What's amazing is that, far from being crushed by the gears of that pagan culture, they changed how the machine works—they transformed that culture! They actually proved to be better Babylonians than the Babylonians themselves: "In every matter of wisdom and understanding about which the king questioned them, he found them ten times better than all the magicians and enchanters in his whole kingdom."[8] Ten times better is pretty impressive, and still they did not compromise their faith.

But conflict was looming. You cannot be a God-follower in a pagan world and not get into trouble. It just works that way. Paul claimed, "In fact, everyone who wants to live a godly life . . . will be persecuted."[9] The question is what will you do? Jesus said, "Do not resist an evil person."[10] The issue of this verse is that we do not have to fight with the people who are vessels of evil— God is with us and we are bigger than that. But we do have to attack the evil itself aggressively and violently with good. Kindness and love and forgiveness and gentleness are the "good" things that mess with evil—like the water used on the Wicked Witch of the West in *The Wizard of Oz* messed with her. And we must refuse to compromise. The violence of a vibrant, caring, faith-filled life effectively disrupts and destroys the evil behind why people do what they do—hence, people and cultures are transformed.

But transforming a culture doesn't come without cost. Sometimes the cost is rejection; sometimes it will cost your life. Think of the fiery furnace faced by Daniel's three friends. What is great about that chapter is the "image" language that is used. Remember that Israel was always supposed to project the image of God into the world, and so are we as the *imago Dei*. Here, Nebuchadnezzar is setting up his own image and is forcing everyone in the province to worship it, including these Hebrew boys, for whom it was a nonnegotiable—they could never do it and continue being Yahweh-followers. It violated their basic understanding of the world. By worshiping the image of a human, they'd be giving up everything they believed in and caving into destructive paganism, which they knew God longed to overturn with his coming rule.

And so, they decide to freely choose the furnace over safety—they tied themselves to their faith to stand firmly against the dehumanizing gestures of Nebuchadnezzar. And, *sweet!* God vindicates them (judgment), and Babylonian culture is transformed (salvation)! When the big Neb says, "Therefore I decree that the people of any nation or language who say anything against the God of [the Hebrews] be cut into pieces and their houses be turned into piles of rubble, *for no other God can save in this way.*"[11]

Through the gutsy praxis of a few Jewish boys, Yahweh shows himself as the one whose

> dominion is an eternal dominion; his kingdom endures from generation to generation. All the peoples of the earth are regarded as nothing. He does as he pleases with the powers of heaven and the peoples of the earth. No one can hold back his hand or say to him, "What have you done?"[12]

And then Neb says, "Now I, Nebuchadnezzar, praise and exalt and glorify the King of heaven, because everything he does is right and all his ways are just. And those who walk in pride he is able to humble."[13]

Through the exile of his people, God brings salvation to the ends of the earth as his faithful few judge and save culture. This idea really is the conceptual universe that gives the cross its depth of meaning. Through *his* exile ("And so Jesus suffered outside the city gate"),[14] the representative Son of Man, the true Israelite Jesus, passes judgment on the kingdoms of the world and then brings salvation to them as he is vindicated by the Almighty.

The Hope of a Different World

Think of what could happen if we saw all the promises of God as invitations to imagine what could be? A world that is "filled with the knowledge of the glory of the LORD, as the waters cover the sea;"[15] a world where the church is "salt" and "light,"[16] which means we make life a little tastier for people and our presence eliminates rot and dispels darkness; a world where believers fearlessly contend against evil and make no peace with oppression; a world where the church consistently uses its freedom to maintain justice in our communities and among the nations; a world where believers imagine themselves to be (as our Savior Jesus was) those who come not to be served but to serve, and by following in his steps we have the wisdom, patience, and courage to minister in his name to the suffering, the friendless, and the needy. *Imagine that.*

What could happen then? Maybe this is what Jesus was getting at when he said, "Therefore I tell you, whatever you ask for in prayer, believe that you have received it, and it will be yours."[17] Maybe Jesus was daring us to actually "believe" when we prayed it was ours—to actually *expect* it?

This would mean we could ask God to help us imagine world peace. We could ask him to:

> Kindle in every heart the true love of peace, and guide with your wisdom those who take counsel for the nations of the earth, that in tranquility your dominion may increase until the earth is filled with the knowledge of your love; through Jesus Christ our Lord.[18]

Imagine that.

Imagine a world free from hunger and prejudice; a world where we see the fulfillment of God's promise, "I will pour out my spirit on all people."[19] Imagine the nations coming to God in worldwide revival and the fulfillment of the promise in the Psalms, "Ask of me, and I will make the nations your inheritance, the ends of the earth your possession."[20] What if we asked and actually imagined an answer?

What if Paul wasn't kidding when he declared, "Now to him who is able to do immeasurably more than all we ask *or imagine*"?[21] What if we dared imagine more? What if we took the thoughts of God—his promises and hope for the world—into our minds (vis-à-vis the Scriptures) and opened up our souls to the Holy Spirit for him to impart God's "fruit" into us—his feelings of: love, joy, peace, patience, kindness, goodness, faithfulness, gentleness, and self-control? Imagine that!

What if God gave us biblical prophecy, not so we could hold the daily news in one hand and the Bible in the other— carefully reading the *New York Times* and the *Jerusalem Post* the way a psychic reads tea leaves in order to find timelines for the fulfillment of Bible prophecy? What if he gave us biblical prophecy so we could have a snapshot of the future he intends to give his people? What if he wanted us to cultivate vision of what the future is going to be—of what the world is going to be like? The Bible promises that a day is coming when "the dwelling of God" will be with people, "and he will live with them." It claims that we "will be his people, and God himself will be with them and be their God."[22] Then there's this promise: "He will wipe every tear from their eyes. There will be no more death or mourning or crying or pain, for the old order of things has passed away."[23]

What if we imagined a world where God always dwells with us and where all tears are wiped away and where all crying and pain is gone? What if we are to carry that vision in our minds? And what if we realized we can do things to hasten this reality? That would certainly explain why the writer of Hebrews asserted, "We do not want you to become lazy, but to imitate those who through faith and patience inherit what has been promised."[24]

Theologians tell us that there is an "eschatological tension" in the kingdom of God—that in one sense the kingdom of God is here, but in another sense, not yet. Jesus told us, "The kingdom of God is at hand," and yet, he spoke of it as coming in the future. It's on a continuum somewhere between "here" and "not yet." And apparently believers have something to do with where it is. Jesus told us to pray to the Father asking, "Thy kingdom come, thy will be done in earth, as it is in heaven."[25]

The Vow

However much of the kingdom we can experience here, we know we will never fully have it until Jesus returns. But the kingdom is among us in some measure, and it can be experienced here now. What if vow-making helps secure that because vows help to prevent "laziness" on our part?

I think the Christian is supposed to long for a better world—one that God imagines. And we start by living better ourselves. This is the domain of vow-making. Like the prophets of old who pointed to another world, we vow to live a lifestyle that prophetically proclaims God's kingdom and interest in this world. We do so by consistently saying no to loving this present world. But our no is not an end in itself; it implies a yes to something more. We say yes to putting our love on something other than what is in the world. In vowing, we choose to ground our lives in values bigger than our solitary needs, wants, desires, and exaggerated sense of fairness and justice. We love and seek the kingdom of God. This is a quest to see God's actions in the world.

So what are you waiting for? Vow into some of those things that have historically imparted grace to you. You will burn brightly if you do, and you will change the world. And email me at ed@edgungor.com. I'd love to hear your experiences and frustrations as you participate in the enterprise of vow-making.

The Classical Disciplines[1]

"A discipline for the spiritual life is, when the dust of history is blown away, nothing but an activity undertaken to bring us into more effective cooperation with Christ and his kingdom."

The Spirit of the Disciplines, 156

As we sort out for our time and place in history just what it means to live a life aligned with God's kingdom gestures, we come to the classical disciplines of the Christian faith. These time-honored and tested practices have been used by the faithful in every age to find life in the way of Jesus. Disciplines like solitude, silence, prayer, study, worship, service, sacrifice, and many more, are activities that followers of Christ throughout history have undertaken in order to orient themselves rightly in God's world and to nurture themselves as his image-bearers for effective participation in the grand motion of God bringing redemption to humanity: the *missio Dei.* But what exactly are those "activities," and how can we begin to participate in them?

We find some help in answering our question from Dallas

Willard in his book *The Spirit of the Disciplines: Understanding How God Changes Lives.* After spending several chapters elucidating exactly how the disciplines are supposed to function in the life of a believer, Willard begins to lay out "some main disciplines for the spiritual life." These disciplines, according to Willard, can be broken up into two main categories: Disciplines of Abstinence, and Disciplines of Engagement. In the former, one intentionally withdraws from or "abstains" from "the satisfaction of what we generally regard as normal and legitimate desires"[2] in order to bring those desires back into their proper place relative to God's kingdom. In the latter, one "engages" in some activity in order to participate more fully in that kingdom.

The following will be a short description of some of the classical disciplines of the Christian faith categorized along the lines that Willard suggests.

The Disciplines of Abstinence

Solitude
Solitude is the bedrock and proper context for all of the disciplines, and it is chief among the disciplines of abstinence. In solitude one intentionally withdraws from human interaction for a set period of time in order to center on God and his ways. The time of solitude can be filled with a variety of activities: prayer, study, worship, fasting, silence, meditation; but at its most basic level, solitude is the intentional creation of space wherein one can hear and remember the story of God and

measure their life accordingly. Intentional, regular solitude is the most basic way one counteracts the pervasive tendency to "be conformed to this world"; it is the place where one can "be transformed by the renewing of your mind."[3]

Silence

Silence, as Willard puts it, "goes beyond solitude, and without it solitude has little effect."[4] Life is constantly "messaging" us. TVs, CD players, radios, iPods cause an incessant stream of messages to come pouring into our lives, many of which are counter-kingdom, cutting directly against the great overarching story that we live in. The twin disciplines of solitude and silence help counteract this and help us to develop quiet, settled, thoughtful, and confident souls capable of interacting meaningfully with God and his world.

Fasting

Fasting is one of the most difficult disciplines for a person committed to the way of Jesus to practice, and yet it is one of the most important, for it is in fasting that we expose our errant cravings and discover how true it is that we have not really mastered the distorted impulses of the flesh but have merely hidden them under our eating habits. We find that we have not truly discovered how to live "not by bread alone, but on every word that comes from the mouth of God,"[5] and we begin to discover how to make the flesh our servant and not our master. As one of the great devotional masters put it, "Refrain from gluttony and thou shalt the more easily restrain all the inclinations of the flesh."[6]

Frugality

Frugality is the discipline of controlled spending. Willard writes, "In frugality we abstain from using money or goods at our disposal in ways that merely gratify our desires or our hunger for status, glamour, or luxury."[7] Though as a discipline frugality is to work through the whole manner of our lives, it can be meaningfully practiced in short, intensive durations as a way of remembering Paul's charge "not to be arrogant nor to put [your] hope in wealth, which is so uncertain, but to put [your] hope in God, who richly provides us with everything for our enjoyment … to do good, to be rich in good deeds, and to be generous and willing to share."[8] Frugality makes space in our lives for humble, generous, God-centered living.

Chastity

"In exercising the spiritual discipline of chastity, we purposefully turn away from dwelling upon or engaging in the sexual dimension of our relationships to others—even our husbands or wives."[9] Sex and sexuality, according to the biblical witness, are good and wonderful things—essential to what it means to be made in the *imago Dei*.[10] Nevertheless, the world, the flesh, and the devil distort sex both by trivializing it and by making it the very center of life. By practicing the discipline of chastity, whether as a single person learning to control your thought life and interaction with members of the opposite sex, or as a married person learning how to place your desire for sex within the greater context of a God-honoring relationship, you bring your sexual nature and desires into submission to God, restoring them to their rightful place as servants and not masters of our lives.

Appendix A

Secrecy

There is a pervasive tendency embedded in all of us to self-promote, to advertise both ourselves and our good deeds to the world. In reality, this is nothing more than pure insecurity and self-indulgence. We crave the praise of other people and so speak glowingly of ourselves and our achievements because in their praise we find satisfaction. When we practice the discipline of secrecy we make it our intention to hide our achievements and our good works from others so that we may attain "the praise that comes from the one true God," learning to find satisfaction not in what other people think of us but in the pure joy of obedience.

Sacrifice

In the discipline of sacrifice, we are "abstaining from the possession or enjoyment of what is necessary for our living—not, as in frugality, from what is really to some degree superfluous anyway. The discipline of sacrifice is one in which we forsake the security of meeting our needs with what is in our hands."[11] It is in this discipline that we begin to live into the experience of relying on God for manna in the desert. Though this discipline should only be undertaken with careful thought and prayer and after one's financial obligations are fulfilled, it has proven throughout the centuries to be a wonderful way of learning that "every good and perfect gift is from above, coming down from the Father of the heavenly lights."[12] Writes Willard, "The cautious faith that *never* saws off the limb on which it is sitting never learns that unattached limbs may find strange, unaccountable ways of not falling."[13]

The Disciplines of Engagement

Study

What solitude is for the disciplines of abstinence, study is for the disciplines of engagement: chief, without which the other disciplines would lack form, shape, substance, and direction. In study we attend our minds chiefly to Scripture, whether written or spoken, letting the message permeate our minds to challenge ingrained and embedded ways of thinking that are counter-kingdom. As we study and meditate deeply on Scripture we recognize, as Jeremiah did, that the word of God is "like fire . . . and like a hammer that breaks a rock in pieces."[14]

Worship

In the discipline of worship we purposefully center our minds and our thoughts on God, ascribing "worth" to him through the use of "words, rituals, and symbols."[15] Worship flows directly out of study, because as we see and come to understand God and his purposes through the study of Scripture, we then are able to worship him not just "in Spirit," but "in truth." In worship, though we may not always be conscious of it, we meet and are met by God, for where his name is honored, there he is. And it is in the encounter with God that we are convicted of sin and brought more into conformity to his image.

Celebration

The discipline of celebration is one of the most powerful and life-affirming disciplines we can undertake. In celebration we take even the most mundane, "unspiritual" things and turn them into acts of worship and gratitude, thanking God for the good things he has given us and reveling in his abundant love. One sees this in the biblical account of the national celebrations of Israel, where all Israel gathered together for weeks of eating and drinking and worship and dancing and celebration, doing it all in the name of God, who had supplied them with every good thing. When this discipline works its way into the warp and woof of our lives, we begin to find that the anxiety, worry, greed, and covetousness that once ruled over us have been replaced by happy confidence, quiet strength, and unassailable joy.

Service

When we practice the discipline of service, we walk in the way of Jesus, who said to his disciples, "Whoever wants to become great among you must be your servant, and whoever wants to be first must be your slave—just as the Son of Man did not come to be served, but to serve, and to give his life as a ransom for many."[16] In service, we set our needs, interests, and desires aside to work for the good of others, lowering ourselves to meet the needs of those who we might otherwise overlook. As the apostle Paul said, "Do not be proud, but be willing to associate with people of low position."[17] When we serve, we are finding ways to, like Jesus, take up the towel and wash the feet of those around us, finding blessing by lowering ourselves.

Prayer

At its very simplest, prayer is dialogue with God. "In the nature of the case, prayer almost always involves other disciplines and spiritual activities if it is to go well, especially study, meditation, and worship, and often solitude and fasting as well."[18] This is an important point, as one often hears people complain, "I run out of things to say in prayer." Letting prayer operate as a function of the other disciplines, rather than having it occupy some separate, self-contained compartment, will give it focused direction and purpose, and one will find that the other disciplines are actually upheld and made more meaningful by it.

Fellowship

There are few better antidotes to the alienation and isolation experienced by many in modern society than the discipline of fellowship. When we practice intentional fellowship with other believers, we open Scripture together, pray together, worship together, fast together, serve together, or simply celebrate life together, letting the healing and sustaining virtue of the Holy Spirit flow through us to other people and vice versa. In fellowship we experience God reaching out to us through others, and Paul's words in 1 Corinthians 12:7 become a reality for us: "Now to each one the manifestation of the Spirit is given for the *common good*."

Confession

The discipline of confession operates only within the safe confines of fellowship. In confession we allow our deepest secrets, flaws, shortcomings, failures, and sins to become known to other trusted faithful ones, knowing that only as we bare ourselves to others will we know the joy of having relationship without pretense and fellowship with nothing to hide, both with God and with other people. As John writes, "But if we walk in the light as he is in the light, we have fellowship with one another, and the blood of Jesus, his Son, purifies us from all sin."[19] Though perhaps one of the scariest disciplines to undertake, confession is one of the most freeing, as one begins to know by being truly known.

Submission

Though distorted and abused in some Christian traditions, submission is one of the great pathways for grace that God has given his church. In submission we recognize the fact that there are some who have gone before us who, because of their extensive experience and faithful service in the Lord, are qualified by the Spirit to be called "elders" in the church. Joyfully, then, we allow their counsel and direction to combine with our willingness to "help us do the things we would like to do and refrain from the things we don't want to do,"[20] submitting to their wise counsel in love and trust.

APPENDIX B

The Daily Office

The following is an example of the "offices" I do on a typical day: morning, midday, early evening, and before retiring at night. How lengthy these times are needs to be decided by you. Mine last anywhere from ten minutes to forty-five minutes, when I add intercessory prayers or meditation to them. It's important to remember it is not the length of these that matter, but your pausing and centering on God that does. And truth is, you may find this wonderfully refreshing or horribly oppressive. If it is a negative for you, don't do it. There are so many other legitimate ways to connect with God. Universalizing one way would not only be silly, it also denies the fact that God has made us uniquely different.

Here are some things to keep in mind as you practice the Daily Office:

- An "office" is the work of God. It is a time for us to stop, slow down, center, and pause to be with Jesus Christ. The goal is the actual presence of God, not just getting through the Scripture and prayers. This doesn't mean you will "feel" this as much as it means your focus and faith will be on his presence.

- It is good to begin and end each office with a few moments of silence and reflection. You may even want to take thirty seconds in between each of the readings and prayers. Peter Scazzero recommends, "When silent, seek to sit still and straight. Breathe slowly, naturally, and deeply. Close your eyes, remaining present, open, and awake. Don't hurry! When you are alone, if God leads you to pause at a certain phrase or verse, stay with that. Less can be more."[1]

- Don't bite off more than you can chew. You may only start with one or two offices a day. That is fine. If it is something you enjoy, it will grow. Don't try so much that you feel overwhelmed.

- You may want to do an office with some others. You can let a different person lead each time you meet, and you can take turns doing the readings and prayers. Read and pray slowly and thoughtfully.

Morning Office

Be still before the LORD and wait patiently for him.
Psalm 37:7

Opening Prayer
Praise the LORD. How good it is to sing praises to our God, how pleasant and fitting to praise him!
Psalm 147:1

Scripture Reading

O God, you will keep in perfect peace those whose minds are fixed on you; for in returning and rest we shall be saved; in quietness and trust shall be our strength.

Isaiah 26:3; 30:15[2]

Silence and Reflection

Prayers offered for ourselves and others:

Global prayers:

For the World:

O God, you have made of one blood all the peoples of the earth, and sent your blessed Son to preach peace to those who are far off and to those who are near: Grant that people everywhere may seek after you and find you, bring the nations into your fold, pour out your Spirit upon all flesh, and hasten the coming of your kingdom, through Jesus Christ our Lord. *Amen.*

Adapted from The Book of Common Prayer

Optional Devotional Reading

The Lord's Prayer

Special Prayer

Grant me, Lord, not to be anxious about earthly things, but to love things heavenly; and even now, while I am placed among things that are passing away, to hold fast to those that shall endure, through Jesus Christ our Lord, who lives and reigns with you and the Holy Spirit, one God, for ever and ever. *Amen.*

From The Book of Common Prayer

Concluding Prayer

O Lord my God, to you and to your service I devote myself, body, soul, and spirit. Fill my memory with the record of your mighty works; enlighten my understanding with the light of your Holy Spirit; and may all the desires of my heart and will center in what you would have me do. Make me an instrument of your salvation for the people entrusted to my care, and let me by my life and speaking set forth your true and living Word. Be always with me in carrying out the duties of my salvation; in praises heighten my love and gratitude; in speaking of You give me readiness of thought and expression; and grant that, by the clearness and brightness of your holy Word, all the world may be drawn to your blessed kingdom. All this I ask for the sake of your Son, my Savior Jesus Christ. *Amen.*

From The Book of Common Prayer

Midday Office

Silence and Centering (1-5 minutes)

Know that the LORD *is God. It is he who made us and we are his; we are his people, the sheep of his pasture.*

Psalm 100:3[3]

Opening Prayer

We wait in hope for the LORD*; he is our help and our shield. In him our hearts rejoice, for we trust in his holy name. May your unfailing love rest upon us, O* LORD*, even as we put our hope in you.*

Psalm 33:20-22

The Apostle's Creed

I believe in God, the Father Almighty,

Creator of heaven and earth.

I believe in Jesus Christ, his only Son, our Lord.

He was conceived by the power of the Holy Spirit

and born of the Virgin Mary.

He suffered under Pontius Pilate,

was crucified, died, and was buried.

He descended to the dead.

On the third day he rose again.

He ascended into heaven

and is seated at the right hand of the Father.

He will come again to judge the living and the dead.

I believe in the Holy Spirit,

the holy catholic church,

the communion of saints,

the forgiveness of sins,

the resurrection of the body,

and life everlasting. Amen.

Silence and Reflection

Prayers offered for ourselves and others:

Global prayers:

For World Peace:

Almighty God, kindle, we pray, in every heart the true love of peace, and guide with your wisdom those who take counsel for the nations of the earth, that in tranquility your dominion may increase until the earth is filled with the knowledge of your love; through Jesus Christ our Lord. *Amen.*

Adapted from The Book of Common Prayer

Optional Devotional Reading
The Lord's Prayer
Special Prayer

Open my lips, O LORD,
and my mouth shall proclaim your praise.
Create in me a clean heart, O God,
and renew a right spirit within me.
Cast me not away from your presence
and take not your Holy Spirit from me.
Give me the joy of your saving help again
and sustain me with your bountiful Spirit.
Glory to the Father, and to the Son, and to the Holy Spirit.
Amen.

From Psalm 51, The Book of Common Prayer

Concluding Prayer:

Heavenly Father, in you we live and move and have our being: We humbly pray you so to guide and govern us by your Holy Spirit, that in all the cares and occupations of our life we may not forget you, but may remember that we are ever walking in your sight; through Jesus Christ our Lord. *Amen.*

From The Book of Common Prayer

Evening Office (Vespers)

Silence and Centering (1-5 minutes)

Ascribe to the LORD the honor due his Name; bring an offering and come into his courts.

Psalm 96:8[4]

Opening Prayer

My God, my rock in whom I put my trust, my shield, the horn of my salvation, and my refuge; you are worthy of praise.

Psalm 18:2[5]

Scripture Reading (Beatitudes)

- *Blessed are the poor in spirit, for theirs is the kingdom of heaven* (Matt. 5:3). God have mercy on me, a sinner. Help me accept my brokenness, emptiness, and need for you.
- *Blessed are those who mourn, for they will be comforted* (5:4). Lord, help me not to pretend but to embrace my vulnerability, humanity, and limits.
- *Blessed are the meek, for they will inherit the earth* (5:5). Lord, grant me grace to trust you and drop my defenses, be approachable, kind, merciful, and appropriately assertive.
- *Blessed are those who hunger and thirst for righteousness, for they will be filled* (5:6). Help me love you above all else. Purge my soul of all polluted affections, habits, and rebellions.
- *Blessed are the merciful, for they will be shown mercy* (5:7). Enable me to forgive as generously and consistently as you, Lord, forgive me.
- *Blessed are the pure in heart, for they will see God* (5:8). Lord, I ask for a pure (clean, uncluttered) heart. I long to see your face, that there would be nothing between you and me.
- *Blessed are the peacemakers, for they will be called the sons of God* (5:9). Lord, fill me with courage to disrupt false peace around me when needed. Give me wisdom and prudence to be a true peacemaker.
- *Blessed are those who are persecuted because of righteousness, for theirs is the kingdom of heaven* (5:10). Lord, fill me with

courage to speak and live the truth, even when it is not popular or convenient.[6]

Silence and Reflection

Prayers offered for ourselves and others:
  Global prayers:
  For Social Justice:

Almighty God, who created us in your own image: Grant us grace fearlessly to contend against evil and to make no peace with oppression and, that we may reverently use our freedom, help us to employ it in the maintenance of justice in our communities and among the nations, to the glory of your holy Name; through Jesus Christ our Lord. *Amen.*

Adapted from The Book of Common Prayer

Optional Devotional Reading
The Lord's Prayer
Special Prayer

O gracious Light,
Pure brightness of the ever living Father in heaven,
O Jesus Christ, holy and blessed!
Now as we come to the setting of the sun,
and our eyes behold the vesper light,
we sing your praises O God: Father, Son, and Holy Spirit.
You are worthy at all times to be praised by happy voices,
O Son of God, O Giver of life,
and to be glorified through all the worlds.
From The Book of Common Prayer

Concluding Prayer

Lord Jesus, stay with us, for evening is at hand and the day is past; be our companion in the way, kindle our hearts, and awaken hope, that we may know you as you are revealed in Scripture and the breaking of bread. Grant this for the sake of your love. *Amen.*

From The Book of Common Prayer

End-of-Day Office (Compline)

Silence and Centering (1-5 minutes)

Know that the LORD is God. It is he who made us, and we are his; we are his people the sheep of his pasture.

Psalm 100:3[7]

Opening Prayer

O God, come to my assistance.

O Lord, make haste to help me.

From The Book of Common Prayer

Scripture Reading

Praise the LORD, all you servants of the LORD
who minister by night in the house of the LORD.
Lift up your hands in the sanctuary
and praise the LORD.
May the LORD, the Maker of heaven and earth,
bless you from Zion.

Psalm 134[8]

Reflection

Search me, O God, and know my heart; test me and know my anxious thoughts. See if there is any offensive way in me, and lead me in the way everlasting.

Psalm 139:23-24

Optional Devotional Reading
Repentance Prayer

Almighty God, my heavenly Father, I have sinned against you, through my own fault in thought, and word, and deed, in what I have done and what I have left undone. For the sake of your Son, our Lord Jesus Christ, forgive me all my offenses; and grant that I may serve you in newness of life, to the glory of your name. *Amen.*

The Lord's Prayer
Special Prayer

Keep watch, dear Lord, with those who work or watch or weep this night, and give your angels charge over those who sleep. Tend the sick, Lord Christ; give rest to the weary, bless the dying, soothe the suffering, pity the afflicted, shield the joyous; and all for your love's sake. *Amen.*

From The Book of Common Prayer

Concluding Prayer

Visit this place, O Lord, and drive far from it all snares of the enemy; let your holy angels dwell with us to preserve us in peace; and let your blessing be upon us always; through Jesus Christ our Lord. *Amen.*

From The Book of Common Prayer

NOTES

Introduction
1. James 1:27

Chapter 1
1. Acts 18:18 (emphasis author's)
2. Acts 21:23
3. Jacques Berlinerblau, *The Vow and the 'Popular Religious Groups' of Ancient Israel* (Sheffield Academic Press: Sheffield, England, 1996), p. 14.
4. 2 Kings 12:4
5. Lev. 22:21
6. Quoted in Berlinerblau, p. 14.
7. *The New Schaff-Herzog Encyclopedia of Religious Knowledge,* ed. Samuel Macauley Jackson, D.D., LL.D., (Baker Book House: Grand Rapids, MI, 1964), vol. 12, p. 228.
8. *The Catholic Encyclopedia*
9. Eccles. 5:4-5
10. Ibid. Vol. 6, pg. 371.
11. Matt. 5:33-34
12. Matt 5:37
13. 1 Pet. 2:15
14. *The New Schaff-Herzog Encyclopedia of Religious Knowledge,* vol. 12, p. 230.

15. Ibid.
16. 1 Cor. 12:13
17. 2 Cor. 5:17
18. Phil. 2:12
19. Col. 4:2
20. Titus 3:8
21. Titus 2:14 NASB
22. Col. 1:10 NASB
23. 1 Cor. 9:24-27 MSG
24. Eph. 2:8
25. Ps. 40:16 KJV
26. Mark 12:30, emphasis added
27. Luke 18:22
28. Heb. 11:37
29. Ibid.
30. Matt. 5:39-42
31. 1 John 4:19 MSG
32. Ps. 80:3
33. Ps. 27:4
34. Pete Greig, *The Vision and The Vow, Re-discovering Life and Grace* (Relevant Books: Lake Mary, FL, 2004), p. 10.
35. John 3:8
36. Heb. 12:25
37. Heb. 12:26-27
38. Acts 13:22
39. 1 Pet. 2:11
40. Richard Foster, *Celebration of Discipline* (Harper & Row, San Francisco, CA: 1978), p. 150.

Notes

Chapter 2

1. Erwin Raphael McManus, *Chasing Daylight* (Thomas Nelson, Nashville: TN, 2002), p. 5.
2. Ibid.
3. John 9:4
4. Ps. 90:12
5. Luke 13:34-35

Chapter 3

1. Ps. 139:6 MSG
2. Eph. 3:18 NLT
3. John 15:5
4. Rom. 10:3
5. Phil. 3:9
6. Rom. 12:1 MSG
7. Rom. 8:3-4 MSG
8. Gal. 5:22
9. 2 Pet. 1:4
10. Gal. 5:22-23 MSG
11. *Confessions* 37
12. Rom. 7:24
13. Rom. 7:25
14. *Confessions* 123
15. 1 Cor. 15:10

Chapter 4

1. 2 Cor. 6:1 NASB
2. Isa. 43:22
3. 1 Cor. 15:10
4. Dan. 6:10

5. Ps. 119:164
6. Ps. 138:1-3
7. Titus 2:11-12
8. Titus 2:14
9. Rom. 3:27-28 MSG
10. James 5:12
11. Rom. 12:2
12. Rom. 6:6 MSG
13. Rom. 6:14 NLT
14. 1 Cor. 10:13 NLV
15. Jude 24 NLV
16. 1 John 2:14
17. Matt. 4:4
18. 2 Tim. 3:16-17
19. 1 Cor. 6:19
20. Eph. 2:7-8 MSG

Chapter 5

1. 1 Cor. 12:25, 30-31 MSG
2. Gary Chapman, *The Five Love Languages* (Northfield Publishing: Chicago, IL, 2004), p. 18.
3. Mark 12:30
4. 1 Cor. 6:19
5. Gal. 2:20
6. 1 Cor. 12:17

Chapter 6

1. Eph. 4:5 MSG
2. Eph. 5:32
3. Isa. 40:3-5 NLT

Chapter 7

1. Acts 17:28
2. *The Book of Common Prayer*
3. Ps. 73:28
4. Exod. 33:15
5. Ps. 63:8 AMP
6. Isa. 55:8
7. Rom. 11:33-34
8. Song of Songs 8:6
9. James B. Nelson, *Embodiment: An Approach to Sexuality and Christian Theology* (Augsburg Fortress Publishers: Minneapolis, MN, 1978), p. 248.
10. Exod. 20:3
11. James 4:4-5 MSG
12. The Peter Pauper Press, Mount Vernon, for THE HOUND OF HEAVEN from The Hound of Heaven by Francis Thompson, Woodcuts by Jeff Hill, The Peter Pauper Press, Mount Vernon, undated.
13. Ps. 139:7-11 MSG
14. Isa. 43:1
15. Zeph. 3:17
16. Ps. 119:164
17. Song of Songs 8:6
18. Rom. 12:11
19. Col. 4:2
20. Titus 3:8
21. Ps. 139
22. Rev. 3:20
23. Ps. 37:7
24. Song of Songs 1:2

25.　1 Sam. 10:6

26.　Acts 2:14

27.　Ps. 37:4

28.　Phil. 2:13

29.　Titus 2:14 KJV

Chapter 8

1.　Phil. 4:13

2.　Gen. 2:15

3.　Gen. 2:19

4.　Gen. 2:7

5.　Is. 14:13-15 NASB

6.　*Confessions* 4:13

7.　Rom. 7:15

8.　Rom. 3:10-12

9.　Heb. 10:7, emphasis added

10.　Rom. 5:18-19 MSG

11.　Matt. 26:38-39, emphasis added

12.　1 Cor. 15:45

13.　Rom. 10:9

14.　Gal. 2:20 NLV

15.　2 Tim. 2:25

16.　1 Cor. 12:3

17.　Acts 9:1-6

18.　Ps. 51:17

19.　Heb. 5:8-9

20.　Phil. 2:13 NLV

Chapter 9

1.　Acts 13:36

2. Luke 9:22
3. Acts 5:41
4. Rev. 12:11
5. Heb. 2:14-15
6. Zeph. 3:17
7. Pete Greig, *The Vision and The Vow, Re-discovering Life and Grace* (Relevant Books: Lake Mary, FL, 2004), pg. 14.
8. Rev. 3:15-16
9. Acts 3:19
10. 2 Cor. 1:4
11. 2 Tim. 2:1
12. 1 Cor. 15:10
13. 2 Cor. 12:9-10 MSG
14. Hosea 6:3
15. Heb. 6:5
16. Matt. 6:10 KJV

Chapter 10

1. Jacques Berlinerblau, *The Vow and the 'Popular Religious Groups' of Ancient Israel* (Sheffield Academic Press: Sheffield, England, 1996), p. 14.
2. Margaret Farley. *Personal Commitments* (San Francisco: Harper and Row, 1966), p. 34.
3. Ps. 63:8, author's paraphrase
4. Isa. 43:22, author's paraphrase
5. Eccles. 5:5
6. Num. 30:2 MSG
7. Rom. 6:14
8. 1 Cor. 10:13
9. Ibid.

10. 2 Cor. 6:1
11. 2 Tim. 2:1
12. 1 Cor 4:2
13. 2 Tim. 2:3
14. 1 Cor. 9:25
15. 2 Tim. 2:6
16. Luke 9:62
17. Matt. 8:1
18. Luke 10:1
19. Mark 9:2
20. 2 Tim. 2:20-21 NLT

Chapter 11

1. Oxford University Press, *The Oxford Study Bible—Revised English Bible with the Apocrypha.* Copyright 1976.
2. Matt. 26:40, author's paraphrase
3. 1 John 2:27
4. John 16:7
5. Luke 11:1
6. Luke 24:32
7. Matt. 10:5
8. Matt. 8:26-27
9. Jude 1:20; see also Rom. 8:26
10. John 16:13
11. Rom. 8:14
12. Acts 1:8
13. Mark 1:36-37
14. Ps. 139:23-24
15. 1 Cor. 14:33 KJV
16. James 4:8

17. Heb. 5:8
18. Heb. 12:11
19. 1 Pet. 4:14
20. Gal. 5:17 KJV
21. John 4:24
22. Gal. 5:17 NKJV
23. Gal. 5:24 KJV
24. Matt. 3:3
25. Phil. 4:13 KJV
26. Rom. 8:37
27. 3 John 1:2 KJV
28. Matt. 10:38
29. 1 Pet. 4:1
30. 1 Pet. 5:10
31. Matt. 10:39
32. 2 Cor. 5:17
33. Eccles. 5:1-2 KJV
34. Eccles. 5:6
35. Found in St. Benedict's Prologue to the Rule
36. 1 Kings 19:12
37. Eccles. 5:2

Chapter 12
1. *The Catholic Encyclopedia*
2. Matt. 6:20
3. Michael Frost and Alan Hirsch, *The Shaping of Things to Come: Innovation and Mission for the 21st-Century Church* (Hendrickson Publishers: Peabody, Massachusetts, 2003), p. 77.
4. John 16:12

5. Packer, *Knowing God*
6. Virginia Lively, *Healing in His Presence* (Grand Rapids, MI: Zondervan, 1984).
7. 1 John 4:18
8. Ps. 139:23-24
9. 1 Tim. 4:8
10. Richard Foster, "RENOVARÉ: Bringing The Church to the churches" promotional brochure
11. James A. Sanders, "Communities and Canon," *Oxford Study Bible* (New York: Oxford University Press, 1992), p. 91.
12. Leo Buscaglia, *Living, Loving and Learning* (New York: Ballentine Books, 1982), p. 17.
13. Aristotle, *Nicomachean Ethics*. Trans. Martin Ostwald (New Jersey: Prentice Hall, 1999), section 1180a:29.
14. 1 Cor. 12:26 AMP
15. 1 Cor. 12:19-23, 25 MSG
16. Titus 3:8
17. Titus 2:14
18. Pete Greig, *The Vision and The Vow, Re-discovering Life and Grace* (Relevant Books: Lake Mary, FL, 2004), pg. 131.
19. C. S. Lewis, *The Weight of Glory*—Commemoration of Charles Williams, 1945.

Chapter 13

1. Matt. 11:12 AMP
2. Col. 1:10
3. John 17:15-16
4. Gal. 5:20

5. Howard Snyder, *The Problem of Wineskins* (Downers Grove, IL: InterVarsity, 1975), pp. 69-73.

6. Phil. 4:19

7. Pope John Paul II, *Living God's Justice: Reflections And Prayers* (St. Anthony Messenger Press: Cincinnati, Ohio, 2006), p. 11. This is a compilation of quotes—not all written by Pope John Paul II.

8. 2 Cor. 3:3 MSG

9. 1 Pet. 3:15

10. Acts 19:23

11. Isa. 40:15, 17

12. Matt. 4:9

13. John 6:15; 18:36

14. Phil. 2:13

15. Acts 2:36

16. Cf. Ps. 2

Chapter 14

1. Matt. 16:18

2. Rom. 12:21

3. Matt. 5:39

4. Ps. 137

5. Dan. 1:8-16

6. Dan. 1:15

7. Dan. 6:10

8. Dan. 1:20

9. 2 Tim. 3:12

10. Matt. 5:39

11. Dan. 3:29, author's emphasis

12. Dan. 4:34-35
13. Dan. 4:37
14. Heb. 13:12
15. Hab. 2:14
16. Dan. 1:15
17. Mark 11:24
18. *The Book of Common Prayer* (New York: Oxford University Press, 1990), p. 258.
19. Acts 2:17
20. Ps. 2:8
21. Eph. 3:20, author's emphasis
22. Rev. 21:3
23. Rev. 21:4
24. Heb. 6:12
25. Matt. 6:10 KJV

Appendix A

1. Adapted from Dallas Willard, *The Spirit of the Disciplines* (HarperSanFrancisco, 1988)
2. Willard, 159
3. Rom. 12:1-2 NASB
4. Willard, 163
5. Matt. 4:4
6. Thomas a Kempis, as quoted in Willard, 167
7. Willard, 168
8. 1 Tim. 6:18
9. Willard, 170
10. Gen. 1:26
11. Willard, 174-175
12. James 1:17

13. Willard, 175
14. Jer. 23:29
15. Willard, 177
16. Matt. 20:26-28
17. Rom. 12:16
18. Willard, 184
19. 1 John 1:7
20. Willard, 190

Appendix B
1. Peter Scazzero, *Emotionally Healthy Spirituality: Unleash a Revolution in Your Life in Christ* (Franklin, TN: Integrity Publishers, 2006), p. 213.
2. *The Oxford Study Bible—Revised English Bible with the Apocrypha.* Copyright 1976 by Oxford University Press.
3. Ibid.
4. Ibid.
5. Ibid.
6. Scazzero, p. 218.
7. *The Oxford Study Bible*
8. Ibid.

ABOUT THE AUTHOR

Ed Gungor serves as senior pastor of Peoples Church in Tulsa, Oklahoma. He is a popular and dynamic speaker, challenging people at churches, universities, and conferences to make a positive and faith-filled impact on their world. Gungor is also the author of several books, including the *New York Times* bestseller *There Is More to the Secret*, and *Religiously Transmitted Diseases*.

WWW.EDGUNGOR.COM

Is it possible to believe in both God and the Law of Attraction?

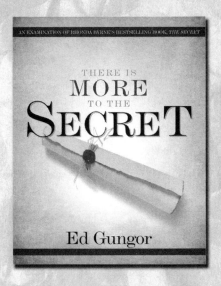

In this deeply compelling work, Ed Gungor seeks to establish a more complete and accurate representation of the power of the mind by explaining the role that God plays in that equation. This book is not written to attack but rather to examine what the author believes is misguided advice while still speaking to the heartfelt need that is causing so many to explore this ancient practice. Some of his views may surprise you. There is more to the story that must be told.

THOMAS NELSON
Since 1798

thomasnelson.com